D1318039

DISCARD

The West Coast
experience.

THEMES IN CANADIAN LITERATURE
General Editor *David Arnason*

The West Coast Experience

Edited by
Jack Hodgins

Macmillan of Canada

Themes in Canadian Literature

The Artist in Canadian Literature edited by Lionel Wilson
Canadian Humour and Satire edited by Theresa Ford
Canadian Myths and Legends edited by Michael O. Nowlan
The Depression in Canadian Literature edited by Alice K. Hale
  and Sheila Brooks
The French Canadian Experience edited by Gaston Saint-Pierre
The Frontier Experience edited by Jack Hodgins
The Immigrant Experience edited by Leuba Bailey
Isolation in Canadian Literature edited by David Arnason
The Maritime Experience edited by Michael O. Nowlan
Native Peoples in Canadian Literature edited by William and
  Christine Mowat
The Ontario Experience edited by John Stevens
The Prairie Experience edited by Terry Angus
The Role of Woman in Canadian Literature edited by Elizabeth
  McCullough
The Search for Identity edited by James Foley
The Urban Experience edited by John Stevens
The West Coast Experience edited by Jack Hodgins

© 1976 The Macmillan Company of Canada Limited
70 Bond Street, Toronto M5B 1X3
Affiliated with Maclean-Hunter Learning Materials Company.

ISBN 0-7705-1366-2

Canadian Cataloguing in Publication Data

Main entry under title:
The West Coast experience
(Themes in Canadian literature)
ISBN 0-7705-1366-2 pa.
Bibliography: p.
1. Canadian literature (English) — British Columbia*
I. Hodgins, Jack, date   II. Series.
PS8237.B75W48   C810'.8'032   C76-017049-5
PR9198.2.B75W48

Printed in Canada

ACKNOWLEDGMENTS

Grateful acknowledgment is made for the use of copyright material.

Photographs: p. 5, Haida totem poles, B.C., Miller Services Ltd.; p. 6, Victoria, B.C., 1860, Provincial Archives, Victoria, B.C.; p. 11, British Columbia, 1778, Confederation Life Collection; p. 13, Vancouver, Miller Services Ltd.; p. 19, Okanagan Valley, Information Canada Photothèque; p. 20, Hell's Gate, Fraser Canyon, British Columbia Government Photograph; p. 21, cattle roundup, B.C., Miller Services Ltd.; p. 47, killer whale, Miller Services Ltd.; p. 54, Bella Coola harbour, Miller Services Ltd.; p. 79, Miller Services Ltd.; p. 105, Miller Services Ltd.; p. 108, Ontario Ministry of Natural Resources; p. 110, Information Canada Photothèque.

Earle Birney: "Images in Place of Logging" from *The Collected Poems of Earle Birney*, reprinted by permission of The Canadian Publishers, McClelland and Stewart Limited, Toronto.

bill bissett: "killer whale" from *Nobody Owns the Earth* by bill bissett, reprinted by permission of House of Anansi Press Limited.

George Bowering: "The Student of the Road" from *The Silver Wire*, Quarry Press, Kingston (1966), reprinted by permission of the Author.

Frank Davey: "West Coast" from *Bridge Force* (1965), reprinted by permission of the Author.

Simon Fraser: "Hell's Gate, June 26, 1808" from *The Letters and Journals of Simon Fraser, 1806-1808*, edited by W. Kaye Lamb, Macmillan of Canada (1960).

Maxine Gadd: "North" from *West Coast Seen* edited by Jim Brown and David Phillips, Talonbooks, Vancouver (1969), reprinted by permission of the Author.

Chief Dan George: "No Longer" from *My Heart Soars* by Chief Dan George and Helmut Hirnschall (1974). Reprinted by permission of Hancock House Publishers Ltd., Saanichton, B.C.

Susan Goldwater: "Metamorphosis", first published in *Vancouver Island Poems* edited by Robert Sword, Tim Groves, and Mario M. Martinelli, copyright © 1973 Soft Press; reprinted by permission of Soft Press, Victoria, B.C.

Roderick Haig-Brown: "British Columbia: Loggers and Lotus Eaters" from *Canada: A Guide to the Peaceable Kingdom* edited by William Kilbourn, Macmillan of Canada (1970). Reprinted by permission of the Author.

Jack Hodgins: "The Trench Dwellers" from *Spit Delaney's Island* by Jack Hodgins, Macmillan of Canada, 1976. Originally appeared in *Journal of Canadian Fiction*.

Joy Kogawa: "What Do I Remember of the Evacuation?" from *A Choice of Dreams* by Joy Kogawa, reprinted by permission of The Canadian Publishers, McClelland and Stewart Limited, Toronto.

Patrick Lane: "Elephants" from *Beware the Months of Fire* by Patrick Lane, reprinted by permission of House of Anansi Press Limited.

Dorothy Livesay: "The Artefacts: West Coast" and "Call My People Home" from *Collected Poems, The Two Seasons* by Dorothy Livesay, reprinted by permission of McGraw-Hill Ryerson Limited.

Thelma Reid Lower: "Indian Children" from *British Columbia* edited by R. E. Watters, McClelland and Stewart (1961).

Alice Munro: "Forgiveness in Families" from *Something I've Been Meaning To Tell You* by Alice Munro, reprinted by permission of McGraw-Hill Ryerson Limited.

Susan Musgrave: "Equinox" from *Grave-Dirt and Selected Strawberries* by Susan Musgrave, reprinted by permission of The Macmillan Company of Canada Limited.

bp nichol: "Allegory 1" and "Allegory 14" from *Love: A Book of Remembrances* by bp nichol (1974), reprinted by permission of the Author and Talonbooks, Vancouver.

Eric Nicol: "First Province on the Left" from *The Best of Eric Nicol*, reprinted by permission of McGraw-Hill Ryerson Limited.

Allan Safarik: "Dream Horses, Plateau North" from *Event* magazine, Vol. 4, No. 1 (Winter 75), Douglas College, New Westminster, B.C. Reprinted by permission of the Author.

Paul St. Pierre: "A Non-Romance in the Moose Country" from *The Chilcotin Holiday* by Paul St. Pierre, reprinted by permission of The Canadian Publishers, McClelland and Stewart Limited, Toronto.

Andreas Schroeder: "The Late Man" from *The Late Man* by Andreas Schroeder, Sono Nis Press (1971). Originally published in *Fourteen Stories High* edited by David Helwig and Tom Marshall (1971), reprinted by permission of Oberon Press, Ottawa.

Phyllis Webb: "Beachcomber" from *Selected Poems (1954-1965)* by Phyllis Webb (1971), reprinted by permission of the Author and Talonbooks, Vancouver.

Ethel Wilson: "I Just Love Dogs" from *Mrs. Golightly and Other Stories* by Ethel Wilson, reprinted by permission of The Macmillan Company of Canada Limited.

George Woodcock: "Encounter with an Archangel" from *The Rejection of Politics and Other Essays* by George Woodcock, reprinted by permission of New Press, Don Mills, Ont.

CONTENTS

INTRODUCTION

In the final poem of this anthology we are given the impression that the west coast is decorated with a long row of modern houses, each with its huge picture window through which the inhabitants can stare out over the Pacific Ocean. The explorers, the settlers, all the west-moving frontiersmen have run out of land; lined up along the shore, their steam engines and covered wagons of no further use, they can only look with frustration out over the mist and the gulls. An investigation of the enormous amount of literature being produced in British Columbia, however, soon reveals that within those ranch houses people are doing a great deal more than admiring the view or resenting the obstacle waves; an astonishing number are busy writing — poems, plays, stories, articles, novels — and many are publishing magazines, literary journals, and books.

Many critics have accused these writers of being concerned with little else than what can be seen through those picture windows. West coast literature, they say, is too concerned with recording landscape: too many mountains, too much salt water, too many pages describing the brooding cliffs and crashing waves. Certainly it is possible to get the impression that B.C. writers are like a lot of Adams gone mad in Eden, naming everything in sight. But it must be remembered that this is, in a literary sense, unexplored territory; writers are making maps. And it must not be ignored that very few of the contemporary writers in British Columbia are content simply to record the landscape, or even just to celebrate it.

A wide reading, in fact, reveals a great deal more. Those who deal with landscape/seascape are concerned with more than just the famous beauty of the environment, and with more than its threatening presence; more often they write with a sense of guilt or sorrow for the rapacious manner in which it has been treated, and with a concern for its safety. A selection in this book, for instance, makes use of the captured killer whale as a haunting and horrifying reminder of man's attitude to the creatures that share this space. Other people, too, are part of the landscape, and much of the writing is concerned with our treatment of each other: two selections are preoccupied with one of the uneasiest events in the province's history, the evacuation of the Japanese citizens from the coast during the Second World War.

There is a sense here that our relationship with the landscape is so intense that we can become indistinguishable from it. It is no surprise to the coast resident that Susan Goldwater can feel the earth's sap sending life up through her limbs to transform her into a green and leafy creature: we can exchange places. And we sometimes wish to exchange places not only with the things of our landscape, these writers seem to imply, but also with each other. Empathy: though many west coast writers seem concerned with only themselves, most seem to reach out and become a part of the land, the sea, the people.

Anyone who lives on the coast could only nod in agreement when one of Matt Cohen's characters says, in his novel *Wooden Hunters*, "This is the edge of the world." It really is. There is a sense, here, living at the edge of the continent, that this is also the extreme frontier of the world. Old realities can be thought of as left behind in old countries (England or Hungary or Nova Scotia or Ontario or wherever) and new realities can take their place, the realities of Lotus Eaters perhaps. Writers here, concerned with the new interior realities of their private visions, sometimes require unusual forms of their own (like the allegories of bp nichol), a logic of their own (like the metaphorical world of Schroeder's "The Late Man"), and a spelling of their own (like bill bissett's). Though many writers on the west coast work within the naturalist traditions recognized by people everywhere, many are experimenting with new ways of writing, new ways of reaching an audience.

Good writing anywhere, though always growing out of a particular region, does not remain rooted to the landscape or limited to a private vision; it achieves some kind of universal appeal and importance by saying something about what it is like to be alive and human, anywhere in this world. The selections in this book have been chosen because they offer, I believe, not only the concern for landscape and the interest in experimentation so common to the literature of the west coast, but also a variety of fresh, interesting, and profound glimpses into the concerns and preoccupations of man everywhere. *This is what it looks like here*, they may be saying; but more important, they are also saying, *this is what it feels like to be us*.

Jack Hodgins

THE ARTEFACTS: WEST COAST
Dorothy Livesay

i

In the middle of the night
I hear this old house breathing
a steady sigh
when oak trees and rock shadows
assemble silence
under a high
white moon

I hear the old house turn
in its sleep
shifting the weight of long dead footsteps
from one wall to another
echoing the children's voices
shrilly calling
from one room to the next
repeating those whispers in the master bedroom
a cry, a long sigh of breath
from one body to another
when the holy ghost takes over

In the middle of the night
I wake
and hear time speaking

ii

History the young say
doesn't make sense
and what can I say
in rejoinder?

The history of this house
if explored
is perhaps only reiterated pattern
being made over and over
by the young now, —

so there's nothing gained or lost
from the not-knowing
from the non-pattern?

  First it was forest; rock;
  hidden ups and downs
  a hill where oaks and pines
  struggled
  as if a stranger climbed
  the topmost pine
  he'd see the ocean flattening the mountains
  the forest, serried —
  below, only the sculpted bays
  native encampments
  ceremonial lodges, totem poles
  and winter dances
  the Raven overall
  giver-of-light, supervising
  and the white whale imminent
  evil lurking
  to be appeased with ritual
  long hair dancing
  feathered masks

And today
  at Wreck Bay, Long Beach
  the long hairs dance
  shaking their necklaces
they do not paint their faces
  nor wear masks
are vulnerable to the whale
unprotected think to find safety
in nakedness

  (in the cities
  the young are wiser

stave off the whale's power
with maxi-minis, fringes, tokens, charms
LONG HAIR)

but history begins
                        the woman said
when you are thirty
that tomtom, time
begins to beat
to beat for you

                        iii

And in this house, look
examine the door lintels
striated cleverly and crowned
by the encircled eye:
egg-and-dart

5

examine out of doors
those arabesques, supporting eaves
leaves leaves entwined
those shingled sidewalls
scalloped leaf imprinted
over leaf; the forest
pattern brought to shape the house;
and turrets high! and branching rooms
and eaves where swallows nest.

And in this city on the brink
of forest — sea —
history delights that Queen Victoria
made marriage with the totem wilderness
the cedar silences
the raven's wing

Now ravens build here still
Seagulls spiral
the hippie children in these attics
breathe and cry
unwittingly
the names of history
tumble from their lips:
Nootka   Nanaimo
Masset   Ucluelet
The map leaps up
                here did I live
                        was born and reared
                    here died

So: Chief Maquinna   Jewitt   Emily Carr

The map leaps up
from namelessness
to history
each place made ceremonial
when named
and its name
peopled!
events shouted!
                here the waters divided
                here the whale bellowed

v

In the middle of the night
the house heaves, unmoored
launched on a vast sea.

HELL'S GATE, JUNE 26, 1808
Simon Fraser

. . . the navigation was absolutely impracticable. . . .

As for the road by land we scarcely could make our way in some parts even with our guns. I have been for a long period among the Rocky Mountains, but have never seen any thing equal to this country, for I cannot find words to describe our situation at times. We had to pass where no human being should venture. Yet in those places there is a regular footpath impressed, or rather indented, by frequent travelling upon the very rocks. And besides this, steps which are formed like a ladder, or the shrouds of a ship, by poles hanging to one another and crossed at certain distances with twigs and withes [tree boughs], suspended from the top to the foot of precipices, and fastened at both ends to stones and trees, furnished a safe and convenient passage to the Natives — but we, who had not the advantages of their experience, were often in imminent danger, when obliged to follow their example.

FIRST PROVINCE ON THE LEFT
Eric Nicol

(1947)

Although Vancouver, British Columbia, is more than sixty years old and its population is nudging the half-million mark, many strangers, including some Eastern Canadians, still don't know exactly where it is. Responsible for this geographical vagueness are several false impressions: for instance, the common belief that British Columbia is a steaming colony in the heart of the South American jungle. Something about the name, British Columbia, apparently suggests a tattered Union Jack fluttering over a few square miles of monkeys and malaria.

As a result of this loose notion about our latitude, those of us who visit other lands and there mention that we are natives of British Columbia often draw surprised comment on the remarkable whiteness of our skin, on our mastery of the English tongue, and on our ability to handle a knife and fork without injury to ourselves or to others, although we never entirely dispel our hosts' suspicion that we may be concealing a blowgun, or carrying a shrunken human head in our coat pocket.

Another popular misconception about Vancouver's location is that it is on Vancouver Island. In Toronto, Montreal, and throughout the United States there are small but well-organized groups who insist that the logical place for Vancouver is on Vancouver Island and who are liable to turn ugly if you try to prove otherwise. Actually, of course, they are confusing Vancouver with Victoria, the capital of the Province, thereby annoying the citizens of Victoria, who resent being associated with the continent of North America.

Victoria, it may be noted incidentally, has gained considerable celebrity as "a little bit of Old England". When a British colonel anywhere in the world is wounded or feels death at hand, unerring instinct leads him eventually to the windswept waste of whitening flannel that is Victoria, and there, after snorting defiance through the local press, he passes on.

Thirdly, there are a few persons who fail to distinguish Vancouver, B.C., from Vancouver, Washington, which sits just below the border and refuses to go away. And lastly, some people haven't the faintest idea where Vancouver may be, other than perhaps a forest-bound clearing periodically traversed by Indians and Nelson Eddy singing excerpts from "Rose Marie". The truth is, of course, that Vancouver lies on the mainland, at the foot of the snow-tipped coastal range, between Burrard Inlet and the mighty Fraser River. You can't miss it, the first Province on the left.

In 1946 Vancouver celebrated her Diamond Jubilee, enjoying a bumper crop of American tourists, a hardy staple which comes up every year. Many Vancouver residents insisted that the house they were renting was obviously more than sixty years old, failing to realize that, although the city wasn't incorporated until 1886, there was a shack town here for some time before that, known variously as Hastings, Gastown, and Granville. Vancouver was so tough in those days she *had* to keep changing her name.

Vancouver became so excited about being incorporated that she got overheated and burned down. But the hardy pioneers merely spat on their hands, a questionable habit, and built her up again. This discouraged her so thoroughly that she has never tried to burn down since.

The original settlers around Vancouver were, of course, the coastal Indians, who were great canoe-makers and who thought nothing of paddling hundreds of miles to visit another tribe and spend an enjoyable afternoon slaughtering the men and carrying off the women. The fierce Haidas of the Queen Charlottes, for instance, were accustomed to paddle south to California for their scalps, probably because the heads were larger down there. The Indians were interrupted in these cheerful pursuits by the arrival of the Spanish explorers, who sailed in and planted the flag of Spain, only to have the English come right along behind and dig it up. For, just as the Spanish were leaving, Captain George Vancouver rowed in triumphantly. (There is no historical corroboration of the story that, as he passed the Spaniards' ships, Captain Vancouver yelled: "How many miles do you get to the galleon?")

Anyhow, Captain Vancouver, as the sharp students in the front row have already guessed, was the man after whom Vancouver was named. Yet, at the time, Vancouver thought he was barquing up the wrong inlet until he saw the Indians' welcoming committee standing on the shore. Approaching the Indians in his yawl, Vancouver hailed them:

"I am Captain Vancouver. I come in my yawl."

"How yawl," drawled the Indians, who belonged to the southern tribes. "Have you any cheap beads or worthless bits of glass you'd care to trade for these priceless furs?"

"Now that you mention it," chuckled Vancouver, "I have."

Thus the morning was filled with gay chatter and one-sided trading until the Indians suddenly realized that they were late for a massacre and politely excused themselves. Captain Vancouver, well satisfied with the site of the city that was to be named after him, sailed away in his gallant little H.M.S. *Discovery*, the prow of which was already dinted from repeated attempts to find the Northwest Passage.

Some years later the Hudson's Bay Company opened a trading post near Vancouver, and soon the traders were busy breaking glass up into worthless bits and destringing cheap beads. Most of the early trading was done at Victoria, which was a lot quieter than Vancouver, where people like Alex Mackenzie and Simon Fraser kept bursting out of the bush every few years expecting to be congratulated and put up for the night.

The next big moment in Vancouver's life was the Gold Rush. We may as well face it — a good many of Vancouver's early lovers were interested in her for her money. This was the period of building and lawlessness, when men worked the mines and women worked the miners. Bands of ruffians roamed the streets, until one day Queen Victoria made the whole place into a crown colony, giving Vancouver a respectability from which the city has never recovered.

Shortly afterward the gleaming rails of the Canadian Pacific Railway came down the Fraser Valley, to stop short at Port Moody, about fifteen miles east of Vancouver. The C.P.R. had it on good authority that Port Moody was where the ocean began, and saw no point in taking its locomotives any farther (they would get soaking wet for one thing). While Port Moody was still thumbing its nose at Vancouver (they never had got along very well), a champion, Van Horne, arose to persuade the company to extend the line to Vancouver, the City with a Future. Impressed with the personality of this virile town, which had just burned itself down (Port Moody had never burned *itself* down — a pretty stuffy place), the C.P.R. extended its line. It was a gay and stirring sight as the first transcontinental train puffed into the station, covered with people and freight rates.

The rest of the story is one of phenomenal growth, of Vancouver's rise to the position of third largest city in Canada. The largest and second largest are two places called Montreal and Toronto, situated inland. There is a legend that when the good people of Toronto die they go to Vancouver. "Retiring to the west coast," they call it, to this spawn of mountain and sea, home of the world's heaviest dew — our Vancouver.

BEACHCOMBER
Phyllis Webb

Because she insists on waking nightmares,
I'm thrown out of bed in just the way
old man night is tossed out by day.
What is there left for a faded star?
I escape to the beach at seven-thirty
and alarm the others who arrived before
to stare at the mountains or cry on the shore.

The beach-cleaner combs the left-overs
of burnt-up yesterday's savage sunbathers —
those are eyes that were her pearls —
he rakes his briny treasury —
Heh! Leave something for me!
All he leaves is sand and stone,
but the sea and mountains casually show
Vancouver has a fine enough view
to challenge the world in any part
where illusionist or obsessive goes
to recover from a broken heart.

Is she asleep now? Is the sun poring
over her speech-wisdom, slipping hot money
into her marvellous mouth?
But why should I care if her nightmares flourish?
Here, I am saved — as full of self as the day before —
with pebbles and stones and rocks and mountains.
I'll scoop them up in a swoop for our favourite local
sea-monster, Cadborosaurus (a little off course),
who ferries hallucinations around these waters
and makes our crazed imaginings outroar
the stupid Lions of the North Shore.
Generator of myth! Denigrator of the peace!
I'll stone your horny back clear through
Active Pass to the dotted Gulf Islands
and way into Cadboro Bay where you were first sighted
and from which you should never have strayed.

Not deep-sea monster myth, nor mother's milk,
nor love built our Columbian bones,
but stones, Mr. Cadborosaurus, stones
made this country. This country makes us stones.

BRITISH COLUMBIA: LOGGERS AND LOTUS EATERS
Roderick Haig-Brown

Flying into it, as most modern visitors are likely to, from any direction except the west, the province is a spectacular array of mountain ridges, seamed and furrowed with snow, more or less heavily timbered on the lower slopes, the deep and narrow valleys floored by the reflected blue or steel-grey of the long lakes. Settlements are scattered and tiny, the few roads to be seen climb out of nothing into emptiness. Then there is the long let-down over the widening green of the Fraser delta, black city smog clinging along the mountain slopes, and the luxurious spread of settlement at the edge of the Gulf of Georgia. At night the transition is even more dramatic, from occasional dim and tiny lights scattered through black immensity to the jewelled glare of neon and mercury vapor and ribboned headlights laid out in a pattern of unlikely beauty for miles on every side.

As a quick impression, it conveys as much truth as any other. But people are living and working out among those mountains, along those narrow valleys, out over the spread of the interior plateau, up the long coastal inlets. The rich glow of lights, the formidable concentration of settlement down in the southwest corner of the province is the yield of a hundred years of men burrowing into the mountains, stripping trees from the timbered slopes, raking the coastal seas, fighting the inland rivers, threading narrow ways through the canyons, chancing cattle among the gentler hills and kindlier valleys. Nearly a million people live on those eight hundred square miles of delta lands and the same lands produce ninety-seven per cent of the dairy products and fifty per cent of the farm value that comes from the whole province. Considerably less than a million people are scattered over the other 365,000 square miles, where the mountains rear up and the lakes form and the rivers run down.

British Columbia was a hard place to discover and a hard place to explore. The first explorers were more concerned with finding a passage to China and the Indies through the upset scenery than with finding anything useful in the country itself.

In fact they were singularly unimpressed with the looks of the place and at times quite bitter about it. Captain George Vancouver, who put an end to the myth of the Northwest Passage in the early 1790s and explored the entire coast of British Columbia in the course of doing so, was addicted to such phrases as: "the shores put on a very dreary aspect, chiefly composed of rugged rocks, thinly wooded with small dwarf pine trees", thus anticipating the scathing "rocks and Christmas trees" of later coast settlers. In June of 1792, among the islands at the northern end of the Gulf of Georgia, he found "as gloomy and dismal an aspect as nature could well be supposed to exhibit", though he was again thankful for the trees which "screened from our sight the dreary rocks and precipices that compose these desolate shores". As a writer he lacked the angle that makes the tourist folder.

Alexander Mackenzie, who came to the province by land, was somewhat more phlegmatic about it all; but even he, his canoes broken and his men numbed with cold and half-drowned, had few doubts about the quality of the first stream he found across the continental divide: "The evil nature of our small river, which we called the Bad River, was such that we were four full days longer in reaching the big water." Simon Fraser, discovering his great river, had rough words for it: "I scarcely ever saw anything so dreary; and seldom so dangerous in any country . . . whatever way I turn, mountains upon mountains, whose summits are covered with eternal snows, close the glooming scene." Even David Thompson, the kindliest and most receptive of all the explorers, had his moments of doubt on the western slope of the Rockies: "The scene of desolation before us was dreadful, and I knew it. A heavy gale of wind, much more a mountain storm, would have buried us." And then, as he and his men came down into the floor of the Columbia Valley: "We are pygmies among the giant pines and cedars of this country, some of them forty feet in girth and reaching two hundred feet without a branch."

This inhospitable land that so overawed the early explorers

was supporting at this time a native population of at least seventy thousand people, many of them in some degree of comfort and security, with a high level of cultural advancement. It took another eighty years, annihilation of the sea otters, decimation of the fur seal herds, the discovery of gold, reduction of the native population (through disease) by some sixty per cent, union with Canada, and a transcontinental railroad to build a white population comparable in size to that of their aboriginal predecessors.

As settlement developed it gradually became apparent that this was, after all, a rich and generous land; there were soft and gentle places among its awesome mountains; the mountains themselves had a beauty that inspired affection as well as fear. Richer than gold and more lasting were the zinc and lead of the Kootenays and the copper of the Coast Range. More valuable than beaver skins were the great Douglas firs and red cedars of the coastal forests and the salmon that ran to every river and stream. Farmers boldly dyked and drained the flood plain of the Fraser delta and found themselves with land that would grow almost anything; others in the Okanagan Valley were soon growing tree fruits of superb quality. A pioneer's life was never, anywhere, made up of roses and rapture or lilies and languor, nor even of beer and skittles, but in British Columbia it had worthwhile compensations. The climate was kindly enough, at least in the southern parts and along the coast. Work in the woods or the mines or the fisheries was a source of ready cash, while the dream of independence in the small farm or logging operation, the fishboat or trapline was never too far from probability. For recreation, there were fish to be caught in the streams and lakes, game to be hunted in the hills. Signs of growth and development were evident everywhere and in spite of periodic setbacks no British Columbian doubted them. Logging companies grew massive with the power of steam and sawmills worked into the night; the "white Empresses" of the C.P.R. sailed for the Orient from Vancouver and the proud fleet of coastal steamships grew ever larger, faster, and more

18

luxurious; mines became richer and more sophisticated, the Fraser Valley grew the finest dairy products, the Okanagan the finest fruit in the world.

It is rather easy to think of the development of British Columbia as a series of engineering triumphs; the Cariboo Road of Colonel Moody's Royal Engineers, the driving of the C.P.R. through the Fraser canyons and the passes of the Rockies and the Selkirks, the Fraser Valley dykes, the logging railroads — often little miracles of ingenuity — the Hell's Gate fishways, the Aluminum Company's Kemano project, the miles upon

19

empty miles of hard-topped highways built in the years since
World War Two, the great hydro projects under construction
on the Columbia and at Portage Mountain — all these represent
a good measure of the faith needed to move mountains and
confirm the impression of the early explorers that this was
indeed a difficult country. But engineering miracles are
commonplace on the North American continent and reflect
little of the individuality and meaning of a state or province.

In British Columbia there has always been a gallantry about
the job and a shoddiness about the end result. The logger, the
province's true aristocrat, stands large and bold against the
background of his ravaged acres. The hardrock miner,
courageous, skilful, and hard handed, moves on, leaving his
ghost towns and tailings and abandoned millsites as scars upon

the hillsides. The fisherman, proud and independent, struggles in the chaos of a disorganized industry. Farmland, brought to full fertility through three or four lifetimes, makes easy money for the real estate speculator. The construction worker manoeuvres his mighty machines in frantic haste through mud and dust and rock to leave behind him drowned and derelict forests, arrogant mills, and ill-planned cracker-box towns. Enormous log rafts among the coastal inlets, the seine boat fleets, white-face cattle driven down the Chilcotin or spread over the rolling hills of the Nicola Valley, tourists flanked by huge dead fish, loneliness of deep forest and mile-high glacier, gold of poplar and tamarack, desolate black of spruce, reflections in quiet lakes, rock and snow reared against the sky, surge of Pacific surf, and watery glint of muskeg miles, all these things, too, are the pictured, familiar face of British Columbia.

Yet far more than all this, the province is an idea of pleasure and rich living, elegant houses hung on the rocks in West Vancouver, money made from nothing, as it always has been, in the big buildings downtown, retirement in Victoria, pleasure boats, year around golf, equitable climate generally, and in contrast with the rest of Canada, easy living.

The other side of this picture is the province's long tradition of militant unions, from the time of the early coal miners to the International Woodworkers, United Fishermen, United Mine Workers, and many others of today. Owing much to British trade unionism and the British Labour Party it has been, for the most part, a strong and successful movement, balancing the easy successes of capital let loose in the broad and fruitful field

of natural resources. From the time of Amor de Cosmos and his war upon the "Family-Company-Compact", this view has had expression in the legislature, though usually in opposition. Without its counterbalance and the determined humanity of such men as Ernest Winch, who sat in the B.C. Legislature from 1933 until his death in 1957, the province would have been little better than a playground for economic imperialists, with the spoils going unfailingly to the strong.

Even as it is, British Columbia remains something of an anachronism. Until the last few years the mountains had effectively restricted development to a few favourable areas. Modern machinery and modern technology have suddenly opened up new areas and these are among the last on the continent available for old-fashioned industrial empire-building. Stakes, in the form of capital investment, are high; but the returns, in the form of long-term claims on natural resources, are almost beyond calculation.

Living out the final stages of nineteenth-century concepts in the latter half of the twentieth century, it has so far spared little attention for much beyond physical development. The pragmatic values of education are recognized in some degree and the university at Point Grey has become a great, though overburdened, school; it is now supported by two younger institutions, the universities of Victoria and Simon Fraser, and by a growing list of regional colleges. The province's greatest collective artistic endeavour, the Vancouver International Festival, has faded into steady decline through lack of municipal and provincial support. Yet the province has better artists in almost every field than it deserves or is aware of, and in this may be the real promise of change and growth. British Columbia has the wealth, energy, and newness to become the most enlightened and humanitarian of all the provinces. If the vision has become blurred in the rush of prosperity, it can still be renewed in the calmer times of consolidation.

IMAGES IN PLACE OF LOGGING
Earle Birney

Where quiet slid
through needled vaulting
iron brontosaurs
have crashed and bred
The steelshagged wolves
have barked and buried
green bones where deer
had arching fed

We tally the pacifist fir   the prodigal
planters put down on the dossier of comptometers
while the freshets are washing
even the fireweed wreaths
from the tombs of the roots   and the spruce
resisters   cut off   are lifting their paling
hands to revolver sun

By the dying creek
a thoughtless poplar
flies autumn flags
for a cancelled fête
The old cold slugs
the covert glaciers
hunch and withdraw
to the bleak arête

And only our eyes can follow the silken hollow
clouds that go gliding away in the empty
rooms of the sky above the children's criss-cross
of match-sticks and over the men and the metalled
ants that multiply in the browning
pulp of the peeled world.

Vancouver Island 1948

NORTH
Maxine Gadd

emptiness
the thrill of this land

on the northern CNR line, 1964
Prince George to the Blue River station
saw-mill town
after saw-
mill town

"Don't know what I'm gonna do
with all the money I made this year. . . .
Maybe I'll buy one of them trailers. . . . "

the mills shriek
over the snow, night time they are
a red blaze under the clear stars

in the rural schoolhouse cupboard
nothing has been thrown out for years,
forms, lists, sporting goods catalogues

a yellowed booklet from 1936, the Predictions
of Edgar Cayce, must have belonged
to that old French Canadian who no longer
plays the violin.
What relief for people to know
that the whole Western shelf of the continent
from Antefogasto to Alaska
is soon to sink
in an earthquake
under all the sea,
beautiful angel of God, all this dead wealth with it
and us
maybe scurry to higher ground,
live thin again.

I JUST LOVE DOGS
Ethel Wilson

Well, said my friend from Vancouver, one Saturday I had lunch
at the Club, you know, the Ladies' Club. I was leaving, and had
just turned the corner of Dunsmuir Street, going down to
Granville Street (that's our principal business street), and there,
right out on the sidewalk beside the bank building, on the
corner of Granville and Dunsmuir, but up a bit, lay the body of
an enormous yellow-haired collie, apparently very old, and it
was all stiff-looking. A beautiful dead dog.

There was no one near but an old lady with a string bag and
little parcels, and she was poking the dog with her
walking-stick, and saying, Poor dog, poor dog, what a shame
to leave it here. And I felt just the same, and I said, Oh, dear,
the poor dog, what can we do? And she said, I don't know,
dearie, but someone ought to get the Society for the Prevention
of Cruelty to Animals. Oh, yes, I said, someone ought to
telephone Inspector Snape at once. (I wanted her to know that I
knew about the S.P.C.A. too, and who was the head of it, and
everything.) The old lady said quite simply, Inspector Snape is
dead, he has been dead for over six months. I felt rather taken
aback, because I'd been so pleased about knowing about
Inspector Snape, but I said, Oh, well, it's no good telephoning
Inspector Snape. All this time the old lady kept on poking the
dog in different parts, but he never stirred. We felt just
terrible, he was such a lovely dog.

Then the old lady said, Inspector Perkins, he's the new man.
And I said, Oh, yes, someone ought to telephone Inspector
Perkins then, and the old lady said, Well, dearie, I'd go and
telephone Inspector Perkins in a minute, only my husband is
sick in bed, has been for three days. He gets these attacks, so I
don't think I'd better telephone Inspector Perkins. Couldn't you
do that, dearie? I was just trying to work that out in my head
when a lady came up in a purple velvet hat. Oh, she said, look
at the poor dog! Isn't that dreadful, and such a lovely dog too.
My, she said. I just love dogs. I'm crazy about dogs. I like dogs
a whole lot better than I like people. The old lady with the

string bag and I said, yes, indeed, we did too, and I think we all felt a bit better after that. But, there lay the dog, all stiff.

This is terrible, said the lady in the purple hat, this beautiful dog lying here dead, and nobody doing one thing. And she looked round at me and at the old lady with the string bag, who kept on prodding the dog's ear with her walking-stick. I don't know why she kept on doing that.

So I said, yes, indeed, it was terrible, and someone ought to telephone the S.P.C.A. So the lady in the purple hat looked very stern and very practical and said yes, that someone ought to telephone Inspector Snape at once. So the old lady and I said, both speaking together, But Inspector Snape is dead, he has been dead for over six months. The lady in the purple hat seemed a little taken aback by this. But, we said, there is Inspector Perkins, and she said, Oh, well then, we must telephone Inspector Perkins at once.

Well, dearie, said the old lady, who was still prodding the body of the dog, and he certainly was a lovely dog, I'd go, only I don't feel that I can. I'd go in a minute, she said, only my husband is sick in bed. He has been for three days, and I think if you and this young lady (she meant me) went, it would be nice.

Just then some young men came up, and they said, Gosh, look at the dead dog, but they didn't seem to mean to do anything about it. They just stood and looked at the body of the dog. That seemed to make the lady in the purple hat very very angry, and she said, well, anyway I am going to telephone Inspector Perkins, and I said, I will go too. Let us go together, I said, let us go across to the Supreme Drug Store and telephone Inspector Perkins on the pay phone. And the old lady said, yes, do, dearie, and I will stay here with the dog.

So the lady in the purple hat and I went across the road to the Supreme Drug Store, and left the old lady and the young men standing beside the dog. The old lady was still poking it here and there with her stick, and she seemed by this time to be sort of owning the dog, and in a way, I suppose, it was her dog, as she'd found it first. And the crowd was growing round the dog, and people were saying, oh, what a pity, what a beautiful dog, why doesn't someone do something.

But the lady in the purple hat and I felt, I think, that we were the kind of people who really do things, though I'm sure I wouldn't have known what to do if it hadn't been for her. Well, we hurried across the street to the Supreme Drug Store, and all the way she kept saying how fond she was of dogs, and I said I was, too. And she said she loved her dog far better than she loved most human beings. In fact, she loved her dog far, far better than she loved her older brother, and I tried to think of something equally strong to say, only we haven't got a dog, and by the time we reached the pay phone in the Supreme Drug Store, you'd think we both hated the whole human race, and thought dogs should be in parliament.

I am shy anyway about speaking to strangers, very shy, even on the telephone, so I said, please do let me give you this nickel, and then you can speak to Inspector Snape — no — Perkins. And she said, oh no, I wouldn't think of it, and I said, no really, you must. So by the time we had talked about the nickel quite a bit, she put my nickel in the pay phone, and got Inspector Perkins's office. He wasn't at his office, this being Saturday. So I found another nickel, and she got his house, and he was away for the week-end, and so was Mrs. Perkins, the maid said.

She was very very angry at this. I felt quite angry too, and the lady in the purple hat said it was an outrage, and what was to prevent a valuable dog from dying on a Saturday afternoon, and there was the head of the S.P.C.A. away for the week-end. So I said it was an outrage too, and whatever should we do?

So she said, I'm going straight up Granville Street, two blocks, till I come to the traffic policeman, and I'm going to bring him right down here, whether he wants to or not, and see that something is done about this, and right away too. She was very very angry. Yes do, I said, because I knew I would never sound angry enough to make any traffic policeman leave his

27

place, I should just make it sound silly, so I said, yes, do, and I will go back to the dog.

By this time the lady in the purple hat and I were feeling very important only she was feeling more important than I was, because I can never manage to feel as important as other people, although I do try, and she set off, her eyes flashing, and round the corner and up Granville Street, which was very very crowded, and I went back across to the dog.

When I arrived back at the dog a large crowd had gathered, and the old lady with the string bag was giving a kind of lecture to all the people, and poking with her stick, and when she saw me coming, she pointed at me with her stick, and all the people turned and looked at me, and I still tried to feel important. But when all the people looked at me, I stopped feeling important at once and blushed and explained about the lady in the purple hat going for the policeman, and all the people said, oh, what a good thing, and what a valuable dog, and wasn't it too bad!

Just at that moment I heard the queerest whistle, you know, the kind of whistle that families have, and boys, like a signal it was. Well, it was a special kind of whistle, like that, and done twice. We all turned and looked, and there, driving up Dunsmuir Street from Granville Street was a large car, driven by a young man, and the back door was open. The young man drove slower and slower, as he reached the crowd, and at the same moment as the young man whistled the second time, the dog sprang to its feet and wagged its tail — my, he had a marvellous tail — and shot through the crowd and into the car. And the boy slammed the door and drove quickly away. The car had an Oklahoma licence. Everyone was too astonished to speak. It was the queerest feeling. A minute ago there had been the dog dead, as you might say, and us all bound together, feeling very important, and very sorry about the dog, and the next minute there was the dog alive and gone, and us all feeling pretty silly.

Well, I hadn't time but to think how funny it all was, and I turned to speak to the old lady with the string bag. But she was away up Dunsmuir Street, walking very fast with her stick. And all the crowd just wasn't there, and where the dog had been was nothing, and there was just me. And I looked quickly towards Granville Street to see if the lady with the purple hat was coming, very angry, with the policeman, and no doubt the policeman very angry too, and I couldn't see her in the crowds of people walking up and down Granville Street. So I went very quickly to where my car was parked and drove home.

And when I told my husband that evening, all he said was for me to cultivate that dog's disposition. He said that dog had fine qualities. But I didn't get over feeling silly for days, and I was so mad at myself that I hadn't even gone into a store and watched for the lady in the purple hat and the policeman exploding at each other down Granville Street to where there was no dog.

METAMORPHOSIS
Susan Goldwater

alone in the meadow
i sense my leg becoming green
a strong thick vine.
the sap runs up my body
turns my hands into leaves.
i feel the juice coursing through me
in new and diverse streams
clearing away old embankments
washing away the silt —
a sound of birds is in my throat.

oftener now
i go alone
and let Time free —
loose my grasp
allowing the hours to sift down
so i may open my ears under water
and hear the planet breathing.

ALLEGORIES
bp nichol

Allegory # 1

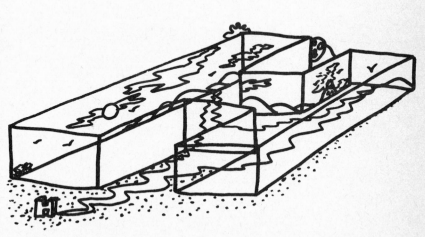

Allegory # 14

FORGIVENESS IN FAMILIES
Alice Munro

I've often thought, suppose I had to go to a psychiatrist, and he would want to know about my family background, naturally, so I would have to start telling him about my brother, and he wouldn't even wait till I was finished, would he, the psychiatrist, he'd commit me.

I said that to Mother; she laughed. "You're hard on that boy, Val."

"Boy," I said. "*Man.*"

She laughed, she admitted it. "But remember," she said, "the Lord loves a lunatic."

"How do you know," I said, "seeing you're an atheist?"

Some things he couldn't help. Being born, for instance. He was born the week I started school, and how's that for timing? I was scared, it wasn't like now when the kids have been going to play-school and kindergarten for years. I was going to school for the first time and all the other kids had their mothers with them and where was mine? In the hospital having a baby. The embarrassment to me. There was a lot of shame about those things then.

It wasn't his fault getting born and it wasn't his fault throwing up at my wedding. Think of it. The floor, the table, he even managed to hit the cake. He was not drunk, as some people thought, he really did have some violent kind of flu, which Haro and I came down with, in fact, on our honeymoon. I never heard of anybody else with any kind of flu throwing up over a table with a lace cloth and silver candlesticks and wedding cake on it, but you could say it was bad luck; maybe everybody else when the need came on them was closer to a toilet. And everybody else might try a little harder to hold back, they just might, because nobody else is quite so special, quite so center-of-the-universe, as my baby brother. Just call him a child of nature. That was what he called himself, later on.

I will skip over what he did between getting born and throwing up at my wedding except to say that he had asthma and got to stay home from school weeks on end, listening to soap operas. Sometimes there was a truce between us, and I would get him to tell me what happened every day on "Big Sister" and "Road of Life" and the one with Gee-Gee and Papa David. He was very good at remembering all the characters and getting all the complications straight, I'll say that, and he did read a lot in *Gateways to Bookland*, that lovely set Mother bought for us and that he later sneaked out of the house and sold, for ten dollars, to a secondhand book dealer. Mother said he could have been brilliant at school if he wanted to be. That's a deep one, your brother, she used to say, he's got some surprises in store for us. She was right, he had.

He started staying home permanently in Grade Ten after a little problem of being caught in a cheating-ring that was getting math tests from some teacher's desk. One of the janitors was letting him back in the classroom after school because he said he was working on a special project. So he was, in his own way. Mother said he did it to make himself popular, because he had asthma and couldn't take part in sports.

Now. Jobs. The question comes up, what is such a person as my brother — and I ought to give him a name at least, his name is Cam, for Cameron, Mother thought that would be a suitable name for a university president or honest tycoon (which was the sort of thing she planned for him to be) — what is he going to do, how is he going to make a living? Until recently the country did not pay you to sit on your uppers and announce that you had adopted a creative life-style. He got a job first as a movie usher. Mother got it for him, she knew the manager, it was the old International Theater over on Blake Street. He had to quit, though, because he got this darkness-phobia. All the people sitting in the dark he said gave him a crawly feeling, very peculiar. It only interfered with him working as an usher, it didn't interfere with him going to the movies on his own. He got very fond of movies. In fact, he spent whole days sitting in movie houses, sitting through every show twice then going to another theater and sitting through what was there. He had to do something with his time, because Mother and all of us believed he was working then in the office of the Greyhound Bus Depot. He went off to work at the right time every morning and came home at the right time every night, and he told all about the cranky old man in charge of the office and the woman with curvature of the spine who had been there since 1919 and how mad she got at the young girls chewing gum, oh, a lively story, it would have worked up to something as good as the soap operas if Mother hadn't phoned up to complain about the way they were withholding his pay check — due to a technical error in the spelling of his name, he said — and found out he'd quit in the middle of his second day.

Well. Sitting in movies was better than sitting in beer parlors, Mother said. At least he wasn't on the street getting in with criminal gangs. She asked him what his favorite movie was and he said *Seven Brides for Seven Brothers*. See, she said, he is interested in an outdoor life, he is not suited to office work. So she sent him to work for some cousins of hers who have a farm in the Fraser Valley. I should explain that my father, Cam's and mine, was dead by this time, he died away back when Cam was having asthma and listening to soap operas. It didn't make much difference, his dying, because he worked as a conductor on the P.G.E. when it started at Squamish, and he lived part of the time in Lillooet. Nothing changed, Mother went on working at Eaton's as she always had, going across on the ferry and then on the bus; I got supper, she came trudging up the hill in the winter dark.

Cam took off from the farm, he complained that the cousins were religious and always after his soul. Mother could see his problem, she had after all brought him up to be a freethinker. He hitchhiked east. From time to time a letter came. A request for funds. He had been offered a job in northern Quebec if he could get the money together to get up there. Mother sent it. He sent word the job had folded, but he didn't send back the money. He and two friends were going to start a turkey farm. They sent us plans, estimates. They were supposed to be working on contract for the Purina Company, nothing could go wrong. The turkeys were drowned in a flood, after Mother had sent him money and we had too against our better judgment. Everywhere that boy hits turns into a disaster area, Mother said. If you read it in a book you wouldn't believe it, she said. It's so terrible it's funny.

She knew. I used to go over to see her on Wednesday afternoon — her day off — pushing the stroller with Karen in it, and later Tommy in it and Karen walking beside, up Lonsdale and down King's Road, and what would we always end up talking about? That boy and I, we are getting a divorce, she said. I am definitely going to write him off. What good will he ever be until he stops relying on me, she asked. I kept my mouth shut, more or less. She knew my opinion. But she ended up every time saying, "He was a nice fellow to have around the house, though. Good company. That boy could always make me laugh."

Or, "He had a lot to contend with, his asthma and no dad. He never did intentionally hurt a soul."

"One good thing he did," she said, "you could really call it a good turn. That girl."

Referring to the girl who came and told us she had been engaged to him, in Hamilton, Ontario, until he told her he could never get married because he had just found out there was hereditary fatal kidney disease in his family. He wrote her a letter. And she came looking for him to tell him it didn't matter. Not at all a bad-looking girl. She worked for the Bell Telephone. Mother said it was a lie told out of kindness, to spare her feelings when he didn't want to marry her. I said it was a kindness, anyway, because she would have been supporting him for the rest of his life.

Though it might have eased things up a bit on the rest of us.

But that was then and now is now and as we all know times have changed. Cam is finding it easier. He lives at home, off and on, has for a year and a half. His hair is thin in front, not surprising in a man thirty-four years of age, but shoulder-length behind, straggly, graying. He wears a sort of rough brown robe

35

that looks as if it might be made out of a sack (is that what sackcloth is supposed to be, I said to Haro, I wouldn't mind supplying the ashes), and hanging down on his chest he has all sorts of chains, medallions, crosses, elk's teeth or whatnot. Rope sandals on his feet. Some friend of his makes them. He collects welfare. Nobody asks him to work. Who could be so crude? If he has to write down his occupation he writes priest.

It's true. There is a whole school of them, calling themselves priests, and they have a house over in Kitsilano, Cam stays there too sometimes. They're in competition with the Hare Krishna bunch, only these ones don't chant, they just walk around smiling. He has developed this voice I can't stand, a very thin, sweet voice, all on one level. It makes me want to stand in front of him and say, "There's an earthquake in Chile, two hundred thousand people just died, they've burned up another village in Vietnam, famine as usual in India." Just to see if he'd keep saying "Ve-ery ni-ice, ve-ery ni-ice" that sweet way. He won't eat meat, of course, he eats whole-grain cereals and leafy vegetables. He came into the kitchen where I was slicing beets — beets being forbidden, a root vegetable — and, "I hope you understand that you're committing murder," he said.

"No," I said, "but I'll give you sixty seconds to get out of here or I may be."

So as I say he's home part of the time now and he was there on the Monday night when Mother got sick. She was vomiting. A couple of days before this he had started her on a vegetarian diet — she was always promising him she'd try it — and he told her she was vomiting up all the old poisons stored up in her body from eating meat and sugar and so on. He said it was a good sign, and when she had it all vomited out she'd feel better. She kept vomiting, and she didn't feel better, but he had to go out. Monday nights is when they have the weekly meeting at the priests' house, where they chant and burn incense or celebrate the black mass, for all I know. He stayed out most of the night, and when he got home he found Mother unconscious on the bathroom floor. He got on the phone and phoned *me*.

"I think you better come over here and see if you can help Mom, Val."

"What's the matter with her?"

"She's not feeling very well."

"What's the matter with her? Put her on the phone."

"I can't."

"Why can't you?"

I swear he tittered. "Well I'm afraid she's passed out."

I called the ambulance and sent them for her, that was how she got to the hospital, five o'clock in the morning. I called her family doctor, he got over there, and he got Dr. Ellis Bell, one of the best-known heart men in the city, because that was what they had decided it was, her heart. I got dressed and woke Haro and told him and then I drove myself over to the Lions Gate Hospital. They wouldn't let me in till ten o'clock. They had her in Intensive Care. I sat outside Intensive Care in their slick little awful waiting room. They had red slippery chairs, cheap covering, and a stand full of pebbles with green plastic leaves growing up. I sat there hour after hour and read *The Reader's Digest*. The jokes. Thinking this is how it is, this is it, really, she's dying. Now, this moment, behind those doors, dying. Nothing stops or holds off for it the way you somehow and against all your sense believe it will. I thought about Mother's life, the part of it I knew. Going to work every day, first on the ferry then on the bus. Shopping at the old Red-and-White then at the new Safeway — new, fifteen years old! Going down to the Library one night a week, taking me with her, and we would come home on the bus with our load of books and a bag of grapes we bought at the Chinese place, for a treat. Wednesday afternoons too when my kids were small and I went over there to drink coffee and she rolled us cigarettes on the contraption she had. And I thought, all these things don't seem that much like life, when you're doing them, they're just what you do, how you fill up your days, and you think all the time something is going to crack open, and you'll find yourself, *then* you'll find yourself, in life. It's not even that you particularly want this to happen, this cracking open, you're comfortable enough the way things are, but you do expect it. Then you're dying, Mother is dying, and it's just the same plastic chairs and plastic plants and ordinary day outside with people getting groceries and what you've had is all there is, and going to the Library, just a thing like that, coming back up the hill on the bus with books and a bag of grapes seems now worth wanting, O God doesn't it, you'd break your heart wanting back there.

When they let me in to see her she was bluish-gray in the face and her eyes were not all-the-way closed, but they had rolled up, the slit that was open showed the whites. She always looked terrible with her teeth out, anyway, wouldn't let us see her. Cam teased her vanity. They were out now. So all the time, I thought, all the time even when she was young it was in her that she was going to look like this.

They didn't hold out hope. Haro came and took a look at her and put his arm around my shoulders and said, "Val, you'll have to be prepared." He meant well but I couldn't talk to him. It wasn't his mother and he couldn't remember anything. That wasn't his fault but I didn't want to talk to him, I didn't want to listen to him telling me I better be prepared. We went and ate something in the hospital cafeteria.

"You better phone Cam," Haro said.

"Why?"

"He'll want to know."

"Why do you think he'll want to know? He left her alone last night and he didn't know enough to get an ambulance when he came in and found her this morning."

"Just the same. He has a right. Maybe you ought to tell him to get over here."

"He is probably busy this moment preparing to give her a hippie funeral."

But Haro persuaded me as he always can and I went and phoned. No answer. I felt better because I had phoned, and justified in what I had said because of Cam not being in. I went back and waited, by myself.

About seven o'clock that night Cam turned up. He was not alone. He had brought along a tribe of co-priests, I suppose they were, from that house. They all wore the same kind of outfit he did, the brown sacking nightgown and the chains and crosses and holy hardware, they all had long hair, they were all a good many years younger than Cam, except for one old man, really old, with a curly gray beard and bare feet — in March, bare feet — and no teeth. I swear this old man didn't have a clue what was going on. I think they picked him up down by the Salvation Army and put that outfit on him because they needed an old man for a kind of mascot, or extra holiness, or something.

Cam said, "This is my sister Valerie. This is Brother Michael. This is Brother John, this is Brother Louis." Etc., etc.

"They haven't said anything to give me hope, Cam. She is dying."

"We hope not," said Cam with his secret smile. "We spent the day working for her."

"Do you mean praying?" I said.

"Work is a better word to describe it than praying, if you don't understand what it is."

Well of course, I never understand.

"Real praying is work, believe me," says Cam and they all smile at me, his way. They can't keep still, like children who have to go to the bathroom they're weaving and jiggling and doing little steps.

"Now where's her room?" says Cam in a practical tone of voice.

I thought of Mother dying and through that slit between her lids — who knows, maybe she can see from time to time — seeing this crowd of dervishes celebrating around her bed. Mother who lost her religion when she was thirteen and went to the Unitarian Church and quit when they had the split about crossing God out of the hymns (she was for it), Mother having to spend her last conscious minutes wondering what had happened, if she was transported back in history to where loonies cavorted around in their crazy ceremonies, trying to sort her last reasonable thoughts out in the middle of their business.

Thank God the nurse said no. The intern was brought and he said no. Cam didn't insist, he smiled and nodded at them as if they were granting permission and then he brought the troupe back into the waiting room and there, right before my eyes, they started. They put the old man in the center, sitting down with his head bowed and his eyes shut — they had to tap him and remind him how to do that — and they squatted in a rough sort of circle round him, facing in and out, in and out, alternately. Then, eyes closed, they started swaying back and forth moaning some words very softly, only not the same words, it sounded as if each one of them had got different words, and not in English of course but Swahili or Sanskrit or something. It got louder, gradually it got louder, a pounding singsong, and as it did they rose to their feet, all except the old man who stayed where he was and looked as if he might have gone to sleep, sitting, and they began a shuffling kind of dance where they stood, clapping, not very well in time. They did this for a long while, and the noise they were making, though it was not terribly loud, attracted the nurses from their station and nurses' aides and orderlies and a few people like me who were waiting, and nobody seemed to know what to do, because it was so unbelievable, so crazy in that ordinary little waiting room. Everybody just stared as if they were asleep and dreaming and expecting to wake up. Then a nurse came out of Intensive Care and said, "We can't have this disturbance. What do you think you're doing here?"

She took hold of one of the young ones and shook him by the shoulder, else she couldn't have got anybody to stop and pay attention.

"We're working to help a woman who's very sick," he told her.

"I don't know what you call working, but you're not helping

anybody. Now I'm asking you to clear out of here. Excuse me. I'm not asking. I'm telling."

"You're very mistaken if you think the tones of our voices are hurting or disturbing any sick person. This whole ceremony is pitched at a level which will reach and comfort the unconscious mind and draw the demonic influences out of the body. It's a ceremony that goes back five thousand years."

"Good Lord," said the nurse, looking stupefied as well she might. "Who are these people?"

I had to go and enlighten her, telling her that it was my brother and what you might call his friends, and I was not in on their ceremony. I asked about Mother, was there any change.

"No change," she said. "What do we have to do to get them out of here?"

"Turn the hose on them," one of the orderlies said, and all this time, the dance, or ceremony, never stopped, and the one who had stopped and done the explaining went back to dancing too, and I said to the nurse, "I'll phone in to see how she is, I'm going home for a little while." I walked out of the hospital and found to my surprise that it was dark. The whole day in there, dark to dark. In the parking lot I started to cry. Cam has turned this into a circus for his own benefit, I said to myself, and said it out loud when I got home.

Haro made me a drink.

"It'll probably get into the papers," I said. "Cam's chance for fame."

Haro phoned the hospital to see if there was any news and they said there wasn't. "Did they have — was there any difficulty with some young people in the waiting room this evening? Did they leave quietly?" Haro is ten years older than I am, a cautious man, too patient with everybody. I used to think he was sometimes giving Cam money I didn't know about.

"They left quietly," he said. "Don't worry about the papers. Get some sleep."

I didn't mean to but I fell asleep on the couch, after the drink and the long day. I woke up with the phone ringing and

41

day lightening the room. I stumbled into the kitchen dragging the blanket Haro had put over me and saw by the clock on the wall it was a quarter to six. She's gone, I thought.

It was her own doctor.

He said he had encouraging news. He said she was much better this morning.

I dragged over a chair and collapsed in it, both arms and my head too down on the kitchen counter. I came back on the phone to hear him saying she was still in a critical phase and the next forty-eight hours would tell the story, but without raising my hopes too high he wanted me to know she was responding to treatment. He said that this was especially surprising in view of the fact that she had been late getting to hospital and the things they did to her at first did not seem to have much effect, though of course the fact that she survived the first few hours at all was a good sign. Nobody had made much of this good sign to me yesterday, I thought.

I sat there for an hour at least after I had hung up the phone. I made a cup of instant coffee and my hands were shaking so I could hardly get the water into the cup, then couldn't get the cup to my mouth. I let it go cold. Haro came out in his pyjamas at last. He gave me one look and said, "Easy, Val. Has she gone?"

"She's some better. She's responding to treatment."

"The look of you I thought the other."

"I'm so amazed."

"I wouldn't've given five cents for her chances yesterday noon."

"I know. I can't believe it."

"It's the tension," Haro said. "I know. You build yourself up ready for something bad to happen and then when it doesn't, it's a queer feeling, you can't feel good right away, it's almost like a disappointment."

Disappointment. That was the word that stayed with me. I was so glad, really, grateful, but underneath I was thinking, so Cam didn't kill her after all, with his carelessness and craziness and going out and neglecting her he didn't kill her, and I was, yes, I was, sorry in some part of me to find out that was true. And I knew Haro knew this but wouldn't speak of it to me, ever. That was the real shock to me, why I kept shaking. Not whether Mother lived or died. It was what was so plain about myself.

Mother got well, she pulled through beautifully. After she rallied she never sank back. She was in the hospital three weeks and then she came home, and rested another three weeks, and after that went back to work, cutting down a bit and working ten to four instead of full days, what they call the housewives' shift. She told everybody about Cam and his friends coming to the hospital. She began to say things like, "Well, that boy of mine may not be much of a success at anything else but you have to admit he has a knack of saving lives." Or, "Maybe Cam should go into the miracle business, he certainly pulled it off with me." By this time Cam was saying, he is saying now, that he's not sure about that religion, he's getting tired of the other priests and all that not eating meat or root vegetables. It's a stage, he says now, he's glad he went through it, self-discovery. One day I went over there and found he was trying on an old suit and tie. He says he might take advantage of some of the adult education courses, he is thinking of becoming an accountant.

I was thinking myself about changing into a different sort of person from the one I am. I do think about that. I read a book called *The Art of Loving*. A lot of things seemed clear while I was reading it but afterwards I went back to being more or less the same. What has Cam ever done that actually hurt me, anyway, as Haro once said. And how am I better than he is after the way I felt the night Mother lived instead of died? I made a promise to myself I would try. I went over there one day taking them a bakery cake — which Cam eats now as happily as anybody else — and I heard their voices out in the yard — now it's summer, they love to sit in the sun — Mother saying to some visitor, "Oh yes I was, I was all set to take off into the

43

wild blue yonder, and Cam here, this *idiot*, came and danced outside my door with a bunch of his hippie friends—"

"My God, woman," roared Cam, but you could tell he didn't care now, "members of an ancient holy discipline."

I had a strange feeling, like I was walking on coals and trying a spell so I wouldn't get burnt.

Forgiveness in families is a mystery to me, how it comes or how it lasts.

KILLER WHALE
bill bissett

" . . . i want to tell you love . . . "
— Milton Acorn

we were tryin to get back to Vancouver
again cumming down th sunshine coast, away
speeding from th power intrigue of a
desolate town, Powell River, feudalizd
totally by MacMillan Blowdell, a different
trip than when i was hitch-hiking back
once before with a cat who usd to live
next door to Ringo Starr's grandmother
who still lives in th same Liverpool house
even tho Ringo offerd her a town house
in London, still shops at th same places
moves among th Liverpool streets
with th peopul, like she dusint want
to know, this cat told me

away from th robot stink there,
after th preliminary hearing, martina
and me and th hot sun, arguing
our way thru th raspberry bushes
onto a bus headin for Van, on th ferry
analyzing th hearing and th bust, how
th whole insane trip cuts at our life
giving us suspicions and knowledge
stead of innocence and th bus takes
off without us from th bloody B.C.
government ferry — i can't walk too good
with a hole in my ankle and all why
we didn't stay with our friends back
at th farm — destind for more places
changes to go thru can feel th pull
of that heavy in our hearts and in th air,
th government workmen can't drive us

20 minutes to catch up with th bus, insane
complications, phoning Loffmark works minister
in Victoria capital if he sz so they will they say
he once wrote a fan letter to me on an
anti-Vietnam pome publishd in Prism, " . . . with
interest . . . " he sd he read it, can't get him
on th phone, workmen say yer lucky if th
phone works, o lets dissolve all these phone
booths dotting surrealy our incognito intrigue
North American vast space, only cutting us all
off from each other — more crap with th bus
company, 2 hrs later nother ferry, hitch
ride groovy salesman of plastic bags, may
be weul work together we all laughing say
in th speeding convertibel to Garden City, he
wants to see there th captive killer whales.

Down past th town along th fishing boat dock
th killer whales, like Haida argolite carvings,
th sheen — black glistening, perfect white circuls
on th sides of them, th mother won't feed
th baby, protests her captivity, why did they
cum into this treacherous harbor, th times
without any challenge, for food, no food
out there old timer tells me, and caught,
millions of bait surrounding them, part of
th system, rather be food for th despondent
killer whales than be eat by th fattend ducks
on th shore there old timer tells me, and
if th baby dies no fault of mine th man
hosing him down strappd in a canvas sack
so he won't sink to th bottom, ive been hosing
him down 24 hrs a day since we netted em,
and out further a ways more killer whales
came in to see what was happening and they

got capturd for their concern, th cow howling
,thrashing herself in and out of th water, how
like i felt after getting busted, like us all
felt, yeah, th hosing down man told me, we got
enuff killer whales for 2 maybe 3 museums, course
th baby may die but there's still plenty for those
peopul whos never see animals like these
here lessen they went to a museum.

We went back to th convertible along th narrow
plank, heard th cow howl sum more, th bull
submergd, th man hosing th listless baby,
th sun's shattering light, them mammals aren't going
to take it lying down we thot, missd another ferry
connection, changd, made it, staggerd
together into town.

THE LATE MAN
Andreas Schroeder

On the morning after the storm, the fishermen got up earlier
than usual to survey the damage and repair what could be
saved. Unusually strong winds and rain had scattered the nets
and flattened gardens, bushes, even trees. Fishing boats lay
strewn about the beach like broken teeth. Everywhere an
exhausted silence hung limply; even the occasional seagull
screech seemed blunted and uncertain. Across the mud-flats the
faint rush of breakers seemed to fade, though the tide was
coming in, slowly and without apparent conviction.

At this time in the morning the fishermen rarely spoke. They
arranged their lines, oiled pulleys, checked over their engines
and wordlessly pushed out to sea. To break the fragile silence of
the first few hours would have been like bursting a delicate
membrane without preparation; it was tacitly understood that a
man needed more time to clear away in his mind the rubble and
destruction of the preceding night than was available to him
between his getting up and the launching of his boat. Even
after they had cleared the beach and set their course for the large
fishing-grounds farther north, the fishermen rarely raised their
voices — as if in instinctive respect for the precariousness of the
human mind launched before sunrise on an uncertain sea.

But someone broke the silence that morning; as the last
remaining boats poled into deeper water to lower their engines,
a young bearded fisherman pointed to a single unattended boat
lying on its side on the beach and asked in a low voice:
"Where's he?"

The man being addressed looked startled, puzzled, then
shrugged his shoulders.

The bearded fisherman risked a further offence. "Could he be
sick, d'you think?"

There was no response. The other man slid his oar into the
water and pushed them off.

A man opens his cabin door and steps into view. He is the late
man, the man whose boat still lies untouched on the beach
below his cabin. There is nothing particularly unusual about

this man except perhaps a certain slight hesitation in his manner; the hesitation of a man for whom the world became at some point intensely suspect, for whom, at that point, a glass on a table became less and less a glass on a table and more and more a thing too strange and amazing to grasp by name. As he stands in his doorway, his hand rests gingerly on the frame, as if constantly ready in case of attack.

About fifteen minutes have passed since the last boat was launched and the late man stepped from his cabin. Now, his boat ready and his outboard spluttering half-submerged, he pushes off and follows the fleet toward the fishing-grounds.

A few hours later the fishing village begins to yawn, stretch and get up; children and fishwives clutter the streets and tangle the air with punctuation marks.

When they return in the early evening and pull their boats out of the water above the high-tide markers, the late man is not with them. During the interval of time between the last fisherman's ascent from his stranded boat to his waiting dinner and the late man's arrival at the launching site fifteen minutes later, silence holds the beach like an indrawn breath. The sound of his prow on the pebbles, therefore, grates in an unusually harsh way on the nerves of the woman waiting for him above the high-tide markers. He has caught fewer fish than the other fishermen.

The next morning the late man appears at his cabin door half an hour after the fishermen have left the beach. Their boats are already vague in the distance when he finally manages to haul his boat to the water-line, which has by this time fallen far below his landing place with the receding tide. He seems somehow weakened, older, leaning wearily against the wheel of his boat. When the fishermen return that night he is an uncertain speck on the horizon, half an hour behind the last of the fishing fleet, and when the catch is scored, he has caught fewer fish than the day before.

Around noon the following day the boats were anchored in clusters to share both lunch and small-talk on the fishing-grounds, and the conversation turned to the late man. "Can't figure 'im out," one fisherman mused, pulling thoughtfully at his beard. "Won't tell nobody what's wrong." "Ain't sayin' a thing," another agreed. "Asked him yesterday what the problem was, but I'll be damned if he didn't seem like he wasn't even listening." There was a pause as if to let the spoken words disperse. Then: "Sea can do that to a man. Catches up with him, it does." The speaker slowly shook his head, threw an orange peel overboard, then absently ignored a deck-hand who had asked him what he meant. The deck-hand finally turned away, assuming his question was naive; he was new in the fleet and often found himself being unanswered. As it was, he was already on the other side of the boat when the old man muttered his answer to no-one in particular: "I don't know what happens; I just know it does. Ain't no man can whirl the world by hand."

The next morning the late man launched his boat some forty-five minutes after the fleet had left the beach.

Little is known of the late man's history, though this isn't realized until he first begins to attract attention by his mystifying dislocation of schedule; suddenly everyone rummages about in their memory for initial impressions, former opinions, latent suspicions, old predictions. Little in the way of substantial information is collected. It is generally agreed that he is a relatively young man, hard-working and "well-disciplined". Some feel him to be a little too much given to reflection, but one suspects this is said chiefly in reaction to his if not exactly anti-social, at least fairly reticent manner. He cares little for other people, though he has been known to go to the aid of a complete stranger for no reason. A slightly more observant villager notes his peculiar tendency to touch (with a curiously disbelieving air) whatever happens to be around him; the remark is received in uncertain silence. Many frankly admit they have no idea what to make of the whole business, and that the man is probably simply under the attack of some unsettling virus. This fails to explain, however (as someone quickly points out), his consistent, almost plan-like deceleration of pace in relation to the normal fishing schedule of the village — by this time he is reported leaving the beach a full three hours after the last of the other boats has been launched.

By the time the late man pulls his boat from the water, the sun is little more than an almost-submerged leer on a mindless horizon and the waves have jelled to heavy, slowly swirling jibes. Night winds begin to cover the eastern part of the sky with a thick, cumulous ceiling of ridicule. Sardonic chuckles ripple along the waterline where the undertow pursues an endless foreplay with beach gravel. The late man stands motionless, looking strangely as if he belongs neither to the water nor the land; his face is a ploughed field but his eyes dart about the beach like frightened piranhas. His boat is a crazily tilted sneer lying on its side in the pebbles, with rope dangling from the prow like corded spittle. Wave upon wave of curling laughter lampoons the beach. Everywhere, everything grins. The late man no longer defends himself. He has committed the blunder of allowing himself and the universe to discover his detective activities, his secret investigations into the nature and composition of himself and whatever he finds it possible to apprehend. But he has allowed this discovery prematurely, before he has had time to properly anaesthetize his specimens, and now, suddenly aware of a spy in their midst, they have disintegrated into countless labyrinthine possibilities and traps and the late man is cut off without the possibility of retreat. He has long since given up trying to sledge-hammer his brain to sleep.

But a violated universe will not be satisfied with the simple deflection of an inquisitive mind, and as if to make certain that such a trespassing will never again be possible, it has turned glaring spotlights against the late man's brain, blinding and overwhelming it with confusion and derision. Stiffly aligned principles and corollaries suddenly go limp and begin to collapse; endless qualifications overrun simple premises and leave behind a shambles of tattered and useless shreds of belief. Above all, the horror is set creeping up the back stairs of the late man's mind that all this is beyond his control, and that like a retaining pin pulled from a spring-loaded wheel, this destruction will continue relentlessly until it has unrolled the tension from the spring.

There appears to be little he can do but to hold on until all is done, and to hope that he doesn't become so weakened in the process as to fall prey to a useless madness.

In a matter of months the departures and arrivals of the late man and the fishing fleet have diverged to such an extent that the returning fishermen see the late man's boat heading toward them at dusk, on its way north toward open water. He stands huddled over his wheel, eyes staring unseeing at the darkening horizon as if in purposeful blindness. The fishing fleet parts to let him pass; though no-one appears to understand, everyone sees the desperate undertow in his eyes and says nothing. When all the boats are secured and the gear locked away, the late man is a dissolving blotch against black evening. A few moments later he is gone.

The late man had returned the previous morning with no fish at all.

As he sat down to dinner, the young fisherman who had asked about the late man early one morning suddenly spoke of him to his wife. "Nobody knows anything, or they won't say anything. Everybody pretends to ignore him. I've got to find out."

His wife said nothing. He looked at her curiously, then threw down his knife. "Well damn it, here's a man digging his own grave in plain view of a whole village, and nobody has the guts to look into the matter." His wife remained silent but a worried look began to unsettle her face. The young fisherman stood up abruptly. "I'm going to find out," he said, reaching for his squall-jacket and opening the door. "Even if for no other reason than a simple matter of self-defence!" he added as the door slammed shut. Footsteps receded from the cabin. Within minutes the sound of his outboard began to move across the bay toward the fishing grounds and the open sea.

For a time the young fisherman directs his boat through thick total darkness; a bulging cloud-cover muffles the moon and the night sways and sidesteps in ponderous movements that are blind but everywhere. The occasional clear splash falls short among the sluggish gurgle and sagging cough of deep-water waves beneath the keel. The young fisherman peers at the bleakness but steers his boat by instinct.

As he moves farther and farther into deeper water the night begins to thin out; his eyes detect edges, outlines, occasional glimpses of phosphoric glitter — eventually the moon disentangles from the clouds and trudges higher into the sky, spraying a fine shower of thin light over the fishing grounds. By this time the young fisherman can make out the dark shape of the late man's boat, lying at anchor on his starboard side. The young fisherman shuts off his engine and drifts closer. The booms on the boat before him are out, trailing thin glistening lines into the water. The late man is fishing.

The young fisherman sits unmoving at his wheel, uncertain as to what should follow. Possibilities dart in and out of his mind, unwilling to bite. He waits, his brain idling slowly, his thoughts loose.

A creak from a rusty tackle interrupts the silence. A glass float dips and scrambles; the late man comes alive and begins to reel it in. A strike.

The young fisherman straightens up and strains to see. The glass float tugs and splashes at the end of a stiff line; the late man's figure curves against the mast, his arms taut like two rigid claws shaking with exertion. The young fisherman feels an instinctive excitement thrill through his body as if the strike

were his own. Something huge is on the end of that line.

The glass float is almost at boat's-edge, momentarily calmer. The late man reaches for his fish-net and plunges it over the side, scooping carefully. His back is turned to the young fisherman, obscuring the float as he brings it to the boat's side. The fish-net rises from the water, then stops.

54

Surprised, the young fisherman leans forward but sees only the hunched back of the late man leaning over his net. A fierce rippling movement shakes the arm holding the handle as something twists and writhes in the meshes, but the late man makes no move to pull it into the boat. Ten minutes pass; the late man still stands bent over his net, gazing at his catch. The young fisherman is unable to see his face.

Finally, in a slow but deliberate movement, the late man empties his net into the sea and straightens up.

The young fisherman watches, still dumbfounded, as the late man repeats the same procedure moments later when another line snaps alive. This time his demeanour seems to indicate recognition or less interest; a short look suffices to make him empty the net again. After a short pause a third float begins to bob and the late man reels it in. Half an hour later he is still engrossed in the net's contents ignoring all the other lines which are jerking at the boom. Bent over the gunwale, his hair blowing about his head like spray in the wind, the late man stares at his catch in silence, then throws it back into the sea.

As a faint paleness begins to tinge the outermost edges of the dark, the young fisherman stands up stiffly, a nervous flutter in his stomach, strangely excited yet uncertain why. He detects traces of the intoxication of discovery in his feelings, though he has no idea what he has discovered or realized.

Carefully pulling out his oars, he mounts them in the oarlocks and prepares to slip away. By the time the sun appears he will be back in the bay and his cabin. Then there will be time to think.

A small sound from the other boat stops his raised oars short. The late man has emptied his net and stepped back toward the mast. As he half-turns to re-apply bait to one of the lines the young fisherman catches a glimpse of the late man's face. He almost drops his oars.

The late man's face is totally disfigured. Crumbled skin, twitching lips, and bleached white hair, he is suddenly old —

an uncertain fool barely able to hold his balance in the rocking boat. The young fisherman is stunned. The late man was of the same generation as the others in the fishing fleet — chronologically about thirty years old. Now he looks three times that age.

But there is no time to lose; the horizon is becoming a thin pencil-line of light across the dark and he will be discovered. Stealthily moving his oars, the young fisherman pulls away toward the south and the fishing village.

As his boat moves into the bay, he sees the first cabin doors opening and fishermen walking down the beach toward their boats. Several of them look up, surprised to see his incoming boat at such an odd time. Obviously his wife has said nothing. He steers toward an unused part of the beach and runs his boat aground.

There, his boat bouncing slightly to the rhythm of his fading wash, he sat on the bow and twisted a piece of rope between his fingers; uncertain, almost nervous, uncertain again. The spreading sun warmed his back as he sat, but his stomach remained cold and unsettled; he felt the desperate urge to run, to commit a violence, tear something to shreds, but somehow he was numbed or simply unable to move. For no apparent reason something seemed to have snapped; his senses coiled and bunched up in twisting knots, thoughts whirled in ever-tightening circles about his head, and a steadily mounting pressure threatened to explode inside him like a surfacing deep-water fish.

Then the faint growl from a distant engine punctured the silence and the tension drained away with an almost audible hiss. The young fisherman looked over his shoulder and watched the late man's boat increase toward the bay. Several of the other fishermen paused and shaded their eyes. For a short while everything hung in suspension. . . .

Suddenly the late man's boat is in the bay, its engine silent, drifting toward the beach. As its prow gouges into the sand the late man struggles feebly to climb off the deck onto the gravel, half-falling several times in the process. Then, hoisting the bow rope over his shoulder, he attempts to pull his boat higher up onto the beach.

Later, after the late man had been buried and the fishermen had returned to their boats, the young fisherman was heard to say that in a totally paralyzed landscape, the only moving thing had been the late man trying to beach his boat. They had watched him for an incredibly long time, trying to raise the bow above the gravel, and when he finally collapsed, still no-one had moved. When they eventually began to climb down toward the fallen figure, the landscape seemed to stretch and expand in every direction and they walked for hours before reaching him. They found him lying on his back, his face contorted with a mixture of agony and amazement; it was the oldest face they had ever seen. So they had buried him, quietly and without looking at each other, and the young fisherman had beached the boat. The next morning, due possibly to the tiring events of the preceding night and day, the young fisherman slept a little longer, and eventually launched his boat some fifteen minutes after the last of the fishing boats had cleared the bay.

EQUINOX
Susan Musgrave

Sometimes under the night
I hear whales
trapped at the
sand edges
breathing their
dead sound.

I go out into the rain
and see,
my face
wrinkled like
moonlight
and long nights
hard under the wind's eye.

The stones lie
closer than water,
floating from darkness
like separate tides
to the same sea.

I watch you
with your shadow
come down over the sand:
your knife is
glutted, your cold hand
has drawn blood out of
fire.
I hear whales
pressing the blind
shore, netted
till I wake binding
weed with water —

How long were you
pinned down
unable to reach
or split the sound?

I hear whales ringing bells
invisible as silence

I hear whales with birds' tongues
and slippery arctic eyes.

How long
did you look

Before their eyes knew you?

Do you remember
the colour of their blood?

THE STUDENT OF THE ROAD
George Bowering

Close rain clouds
hang half way down the mountains
here beside the road
at Hope junction of no hope

and rain impends
cold in the air above

I wait twelve hours on the road
rucksack crooked in gravel beside me
as cars with far away license plates
go by and far away

Silly looking student of the road
trying to roll cigarettes in the wind
my hand that makes the hours and the cars
go by

sun tanned men from Minnesota
look at me, comfortable
in their cars

I feel the light fading
and know I will sleep
somewhere, under a tree

Or I will now retrace my twelve hours
back to Vancouver
and try to move South instead
smiling by the side of the road
to San Francisco

ENCOUNTER WITH AN ARCHANGEL
George Woodcock

When my wife and I returned to Canada in the spring of 1949, I found that on Vancouver Island, where we settled, there was a small group of Doukhobors who had migrated from the interior of British Columbia and had founded a colony at Hilliers, sixty miles north of the village where we were clearing land and carpentering a house in search of that Tolstoyan *ignis fatuus*, the marriage of manual and mental work.

The people of our village talked reluctantly about the Hilliers community, yet even their rare hostile comments told us something. The leader of the group — a heretical offshoot — was a prophet who called himself Michael the Archangel. He openly preached the destruction of marriage, and this our neighbours vaguely envisaged as a complex and orgiastic pattern of shacking-up which provoked and offended their Presbyterian imagination at one and the same time.

Since Hilliers was near, we could easily go there to see for ourselves, but we knew already that chronic bad relations with the Canadian authorities had made the Doukhobors distrustful of strangers. However, I wrote to the community, and by return I received a letter from the secretary, whose name was Joe. He not only welcomed my interest, but invited us to stay at Hilliers as long as we wished. I was a little surprised at the enthusiastic tone of his letter, but the reason became evident once we reached Hilliers.

One day in August we set off northward. For lack of money, we hitch-hiked, and it was late afternoon when the last driver turned off the sea-coast road into the broad valley, hot and still of air, where Hilliers lies in the lee of the hard mountain spine that runs down the length of Vancouver Island. The older, non-Doukhobor Hilliers was a whistle-stop on the island railway, and the entrance to the community stood opposite a siding filled with boxcars. A high cedar fence faced the road. A large board had been nailed to it. UNION OF SPIRITUAL COMMUNITIES OF CHRIST, it said, in Russian and English. The wide gates stood open; looking between them, the eye encompassed and then recognized with some surprise the unconscious faithfulness with which a Russian village of the Chekhov era had been reproduced. Low cabins of logs and unpainted shakes were scattered along a faintly marked trail that ran between grass verges to end, a furlong on, at two larger two-storeyed houses standing against the brown background of the mountains, with the grey bubble of a communal baking oven between them. Each cabin was surrounded by a picketed garden, where green rows of vegetables and raspberry canes ran over the black earth in neatly weeded symmetry, and ranks of sunflowers lolled their brown and yellow masks towards the light.

An old woman with a white kerchief shading her face was hoeing very slowly in the nearest garden. She was the only person in sight, and I went up to her fence. Could she tell me where to find Joe? Her English was so broken that I could not follow what she was trying to tell me. By this time our arrival had been noticed in the cabins, and a little wave of younger women in bright full petticoats, and of blond, crop-headed small boys, came towards us hesitantly. There was nothing of the welcome we had expected. Inge spoke to one of the women. "Joe ain't here," she answered. "He's at the other place." She waved vaguely northward. A pick-up truck drove in through the gates, and two young men got out. The women called to them, and they talked together in rapid, anxious Russian. Then one man got back into the truck and drove off, while the other came up to us. He was dark and nervous, dressed in an old blue serge suit with chaff whitening the wrinkles. "I'm Pete," he said, "Joe's brother. Joe's coming." He paused. "Afterwards . . . you'll see Michael . . . Michael Archangel," he added hesitantly, and then fell silent. The small boys gave up interest and went to play on the boxcars.

Joe was so different from Pete that it was hard to believe them brothers — blue-eyed, wiry, jumping out of the truck to run and pump our hands. "Michael Archangel knew you were coming. A long time ago," he shouted. I had written only a week before. "A long time ago?" I asked. Joe looked at me and then laughed. "Yes, before you wrote!" Then he grabbed our rucksacks, helped us into the truck, and drove wildly for a couple of miles along a rough track beside the railway to a large old farm house in a quadrangle of shacks and barns surrounded by propped-up apple trees that were ochre-yellow with lichen. "This is the other place," Joe explained. "Most of the young people stay here. The old 'uns live up there with Michael Archangel."

We went into the kitchen. Two young women, fair and steatopygous as Doukhobor beauties are expected to be, were preparing the evening meal. A small girl showed us to our room, and stood, avid with curiosity, while we unpacked our rucksacks and washed our faces. Then Joe took us around the yard, showed us the new bakehouse on which a hawk-faced old man like a Circassian bandit was laying bricks, and tried to entice us into the bathhouse. I looked through the doorway and saw naked people moving like the damned in the clouds of steam that puffed up whenever a bucket of water was thrown on the hot stones. In a couple of seconds I withdrew, gasping for breath. The bricklayer laughed. "You never make a Doukhobor," he said. "Add ten years to your life," said Joe coaxingly.

When everyone stood in a circle around the great oval table for the communal meal we began to see the kind of people the Doukhobors were. There were twenty of them, singing in the half-Caucasian rhythm that penetrates Doukhobor music, the women high and nasal, the men resonant as bells. Most had Slavonic features, their breadth emphasized among the women by the straight fringes in which their hair was cut across the forehead. But a few, like the bricklayer, were so unRussian as to suggest that Doukhobors had interbred with Caucasian Moslems during their long exile in the mountains before they came to Canada. They sang of Siberian and Canadian prisons, of martyrs and heroes in the faith. "Rest at last, ye eagles of courage, rest at last in the arms of God," they boomed and shrilled.

63

The singing was solemn, but afterwards the mood changed at once and the meal went on with laughter and loud Russian talk; now and then our neighbours would break off repentantly to translate for our benefit. The food was vegetarian, but the best of its kind I have ever tasted; bowls of purple borscht, dashed with white streaks of cream, and then casha, made with millet and butter, and vegetables cooked in oil, and pirogi stuffed with cheese and beans and blackberries, and eaten with great scoops of sour cream. Slices of black bread passed around the table, cut from a massive square loaf that stood in the middle, beside the salt of hospitality, and the meal ended with huckleberries and cherries.

Afterwards Joe and Pete took us to drink tea in a room they used as an office. It was furnished with a table and benches of thick hand-adzed cedar, but a big blue enamel teapot served instead of a samovar. This was the first of a series of long conversations in which the ideas of the community were imparted to us, principally by Joe, who spoke English more fluently than anyone else at Hilliers. Except for a few phrases, the details of the dialogues have become blurred in my memory during the thirteen years that have passed since then, but this, in substance, is what we were told on the first evening.

The community began with the experiences of Michael Verigin, a backsliding Doukhobor. Michael had left his home in the mountains, opened a boarding-house for Russians in Vancouver, and prospered there. After a few years Michael began to feel the malaise which many Doukhobors experience when they go from their villages into the acquisitive outside world, and he returned to the mountain valley of Krestova. Krestova is the Mecca of the Sons of Freedom, the fire-raising and nude-parading radical wing of the Doukhobor sect. Michael rejoined the Sons of Freedom and was regarded with deference because he bore the holy name of Verigin and was a distant cousin of Peter the Lordly, the Living Christ who presided over the Doukhobors' first years in Canada, and died mysteriously in a train explosion during the 1920s.

"Then Michael had a vision."

"A dream?"

"No, a vision. He was awake, and he said there was a voice and a presence."

"He saw nothing?"

"That time he didn't. The vision told him he was no longer Mike Verigin. Michael the Archangel had gone into him. He was the same man, but the Archangel as well."

"How did he know it was a real vision?"

"He just knew." Joe looked at me with the imperturbable blue-eyed confidence of a man used to assessing the authenticity of supernatural messages. "The vision said Michael must prepare the world for the Second Coming."

The Second Coming did not mean the return of Christ. According to Doukhobor beliefs, Christ is returning all the time in various forms. The Second Coming meant the establishment of God's earthly kingdom and the end of time and mortality.

As the chosen pioneers in this great mission, the Doukhobors must purify themselves. The Archangel began by proclaiming that they must renounce not only meat and alcohol, but also tobacco and musical instruments. A radio was playing loudly in the kitchen as Joe explained this. "That's O.K.," he reassured us. "A radio ain't a musical instrument."

Above all, the lust for possession must be rooted out. This meant not only a return to the traditional communistic economy from which the Doukhobors had lapsed under evil Canadian influences, but also the destruction of that inner citadel of possession, marriage. No person must have rights over another, either parental or marital. Women must be liberated, sexual relations must be free, families must wither away.

Two or three hundred of the Sons of Freedom, mostly seasoned old veterans of the nude marches and the pre-war internment on Piers Island, accepted the Archangel's teaching. Their neighbours showed disagreement by burning down the houses of those who followed Verigin. At this point the

Archangel very conveniently had another vision.

Two of his followers must visit Vancouver Island. There they would find a town where a clock had stopped at half-past two, and then they must proceed eastward until they saw a white horse by the gate of a farm. Joe and another man went on the expedition. They found the clock at Port Alberni, and the horse by the gate of a three-hundred-acre farm that was up for sale at a knockdown price. And, for what the fact is worth, I should record that after I had heard Joe's story I happened to visit Port Alberni, and there, on the tower of a fire-hall, I saw a dummy clock whose painted hands stood unmoving at half-past two.

The farm was bought with the pooled resources of the faithful, and Michael the Archangel led two hundred of his disciples on the exodus to Vancouver Island. Immediately after leaving the mainland he added to all the other prohibitions a ban on sexual intercourse — to conserve energies for the great task of spiritual regeneration. Complete freedom was only to be won by complete self-control. So much for the stories of Free Love rampant!

I wanted to find out the actual nature of the power that enabled Michael the Archangel to impose such restrictions. Tolstoy once thought that, because they opposed the state, the Doukhobors lived without rulers. Other writers had suggested that the Living Christs, like Peter the Lordly Verigin and his son Peter the Purger, had been rulers as powerful as any earthly governor.

"He is just our spiritual leader," Joe explained blandly.

"But he still seems to have a big say in your practical affairs."

"It depends on what you mean by *say*. He gives no orders. We are free men. We don't obey anybody. But he gives us advice."

"Do you always accept it?"

"If we know what's good for us, we do."

"Why?"

"Because we know Michael the Archangel is always right."

"How do you know?"

"We just know."

The next day we met the Archangel. He had sent a message early that morning summoning us to his presence, and Joe drove us to the hamlet where we had arrived originally. The Archangel's house was one of the larger buildings, but we were not allowed to go in. We waited outside. The Archangel would meet us in the garden.

A tall man in his late fifties came stepping heavily between the zinnia borders. A heavy paunch filled his knitted sweater, and his shining bald head loosened into a coarse, flushed face with a potato nose, a sandy moustache, and small eyes that glinted out of puffy sockets. It was a disappointing encounter. The Archangel bowed in the customary Doukhobor manner, but without the warmth most Doukhobors put into their greeting. He shook hands limply. He spoke a few sentences in Russian, welcoming us and wishing us good health, and he affected not to understand English, though we learned later that he was effectively bilingual. He picked two small pink roses from a briar that ran along the fence and gave one to each of us. In five minutes he was gone, retiring with dignified adroitness and leaving all our intended questions about archangelic power unanswered. Joe led us away, loudly declaring that the Archangel had been delighted with us, and that he had given many messages which he, Joe, would transmit in due course. Our whole relationship with the Archangel took on this elusive, indirect form, with Joe acting like a voluble priest interpreting and embellishing the laconic banalities of the oracle.

For the rest of the second day we wandered around the community, talking to the people we encountered. I pumped the handle of a primitive hand washing-machine, and learned from the girl I helped a curious instance of Doukhobor double-think. A spaniel bitch trotted over the yard, followed by a single pup. "She had four," the girl volunteered. "Did you give the rest away?" "No, they were drowned." "I thought you didn't believe in killing." "We didn't kill 'em. That Mountie sergeant drowned 'em for us." She chuckled, and quite obviously felt no guilt for merely condoning a killing someone else had carried out.

Under the prophetic discipline there were certainly signs of strain. I found empty beer bottles under the bushes in a corner of one Doukhobor field, and in the shelter of the ten-feet plumes of corn which were the community's pride a young man begged a cigarette and smoked in hasty gulps to finish it before anyone came into sight. Yet there was also an atmosphere of dogged devotion. Much of the land had been irrigated, and it was growing heavier crops of corn and tomatoes and vegetables than any of the neighbouring farms, while the houses were surrounded by rows of hotbeds and cold frames where melons and gherkins ripened. The younger people talked constantly of schemes for new kinds of cultivation and for starting up light industries, but the younger people were so few. There were too many children, too many old visionaries.

Sunday was the climax of our visit. Our arrival had coincided with the community's first great festival. In the afternoon the only child so far born there was to be handed over to the care of the community as a symbolic demonstration against conventional ideas of motherhood and the family. Since the Archangel had forbidden fornication, we were rather surprised that a child whose very presence seemed to defy his will should be so honoured. From my attempts to discuss the situation I gained an impression that the Doukhobors applied a rather Dostoevskian equation — considering that, if the ban itself was sacred, so must be the sin against it. "Free men ain't bound by reason," as one young man rather unanswerably concluded a discussion on this point.

The day began with morning service in the bare meeting house. Flowers and plates of red apples had been brought in, and the sunlight played over the white head-shawls and bright cotton dresses of the women. Bread and salt stood symbolically on the small central table, and also a great ewer of water from which anybody who happened to feel thirsty would stop and drink as the service went on. The women ranged to the right of the table and the men to the left. On entering the hall each person bowed low from the waist, and the bow was returned by the whole assembly; the salutation was not to the man, but to the God within him. The Archangel stood at the head of the men, benign and copiously sweating; despite his celestial nature, he did not attempt to offend Doukhobor precedent by acting like a priest. Today, in fact, as a child was to be the centre of the festival, the children led off the service, choosing and starting in their sharp, clear voices the Doukhobor psalms and hymns for the day. Almost every part of the service was sung, and the wild and wholly incomprehensible chanting of the two hundred people in the small meeting house produced in us an extraordinary sense of exaltation such as I have only experienced once since then, in a church full of Zapotec peasants at a festival south of Oaxaca. At the end of the service, we all linked arms at the elbows and kissed each other's cheeks, first right then left, in traditional token of forgiveness.

Later in the day we re-assembled in the open air, forming a great V with the bread and salt at the apex. The singing rose like a fountain of sound among the drooping cedar trees, and between lines of women waving flowers and men waving green boughs the mother carried her child to the table. She was one of the young women we had met at the farmhouse on our arrival. As she stood there, her fair face grave and melancholy within the white frame of her head-shawl, she looked like the dolorous mother of some naive ikon. The singing ended, the old hawk-faced bricklayer prayed before the table, and the mother, showing no emotion, handed the child to another of the women. The Archangel began to speak, in high, emotional tones; Pete, standing beside me, translated. The child would be named Angel Gabriel. The fruit of sin, he contained the seed of celestial nature. It was he who would fulfil the great destiny of the Doukhobors and lead mankind back on the great journey to lost Eden.

The women brought out pitchers of kvass and walked among the people as the orators began to speak. Emblematic banners were unfurled before the assembly. One, representing women dragging the ploughs that broke the prairies during the hard early days of the sect in Canada, was meant to celebrate the coming liberation of the sect from all forms of bondage. Another, covered with images of clocks and other symbols of time, was carefully expounded by the Archangel, who found in it the fatal dates that charted the destiny of the world. Then everyone spoke who wished — elders and young women; a Communist lawyer who had come in from the blue; even I, under moral coercion, as the enquiring Tolstoyan I then was. It was hot and tedious work as the sun beat down into the bowl among the mountains and Sunday trippers from Qualicum Beach gazed in astonishment through the palisades.

We walked back to the farmhouse with a Canadian woman who had married into the Doukhobors. "You've seen what Mike wants you to see," she said, bitterly. "You don't know all there is to know about that girl. Today they've taken her child. Now she'll go to stay up in Mike's house. They won't let her talk to anyone, and they'll pay her out in every way they can for having a child by her own husband. Purification! That's what they talk about. I call it prison!" The mother of the Angel Gabriel was not at the evening meal, and we never saw her again. We asked Joe what had happened to her. She had gone willingly into seclusion, he answered, for her own good, of course.

Indeed, Joe had much more important things to talk about in that last conversation. "You have a great part to play in the future of mankind." He fixed me with a sharp, pale eye. "Michael's vision has told him that the end of the world is very near. Now we have to gather into Jerusalem the hundred and forty-four thousand true servants of God mentioned in the Book of Revelation. This time Jerusalem will be right here."

"Here? On Vancouver Island?"

"On this very spot."

"But how do you *know*?"

"We ain't worrying. We just know. And the Archangel had a vision about you. He knew you were coming a long time ago.

70

He knew you were a writer. He knew you were being sent here so you could tell the world what we're doing."

I must have looked at him very dubiously for he flapped his hands reassuringly. "I ain't asking you to do it. Nor is Archangel. We just know you will. You'll write about us, and people will come to us, and then you will come back and be marked with the sign and live for ever among the servants of God."

We left the next day. The Archangel saw us once more in his garden, gave us a white rose each, and said we should meet again before long. "It's a prophecy," Joe whispered.

And indeed it was. One day, months later, I was broadcasting in Vancouver when Ross McLean, who was then a radio producer, said he had heard Joe was locked up in the court house. I went over, but I could not see him. The Mounties were holding him incomunicado. But as I was leaving the station Michael the Archangel was brought in, and for a couple of minutes, in that grim barred room, I was allowed to talk to him. He was pleased to be recognized, and even willing to talk a little English. "I am free soon," he said, as he was led away to the cells. Not long afterwards he and Joe were sentenced on some rather nebulous charges of disturbing public order. And a few months later Michael the Archangel Verigin died in jail.

Ten years afterwards we drove through Hilliers, turning off our road on a nostalgic impulse. The palisade was still there, opposite the railway siding, and for a moment everything looked unchanged. But inside, where Jerusalem should have been rising, there was only the ghost of what we had seen on the day the Angel Gabriel was named. Most of the buildings had gone, but falling fences and squares of thistles still marked out the theocracy where the Archangel had ruled.

CALL MY PEOPLE HOME
Dorothy Livesay

(A Documentary Poem for Radio)

ANNOUNCER:
Now after thirty years come from a far island
Of snow and cherry blossoms, holy mountains,
To make a home near water, near
The blue Pacific; newcomers and strangers
Circled again and shaped by snow-white mountains,
These put down their roots, the Isseis:*
the older generation. This is their story.

CHORUS OF ISSEIS:
Home, they say, is where the heart is:
Transplanted walls, and copper-coloured gardens
Or where the cherry bough can blow
Against your pain, and blow it cool again —
This they call home.

But for ourselves we learned
How home was not
Even the small plot, raspberry laden
Nor shack on stilts, stooping over the water,
Nor the brown Fraser's whirl,
Sucking the salmon upward.

Home was the uprooting:
The shiver of separation
Despair for our children
Fear for our future.

Home was the finding of a dry land
Bereft of water or rainfall
Where water is cherished
Where our tears made channels
And became irrigation.

Home was in watching:
The fruit growing and pushing

*Isseis — generation born in Japan.

So painfully watered;
The timber hewn down
The mill run completed.

Home was in waiting:
For new roots holding
For young ones branching
For our yearning fading . . .

ANNOUNCER:
His ancestors had lived near water
Been fishermen under Fujiyama's shadow.
Each season in the new land found him struggling
Against the uncertain harvest of the sea,
The uncertain temper of white fishermen
Who hungered also, who had mouths to feed.
So these men cut his share
From half to one-eighth of the fishing fleet:
But still he fished, finding the sea his friend.

THE FISHERMAN:
Home was my boat: T.K. 2930 —
Wintering on the Skeena with my nets
Cast up and down the river, to lure and haul
The dogfish. (His oil, they said, was needed overseas
For children torn from home, from a blitzed town.)
We made good money, and the sockeye run
That summer had outdone all the remembered seasons.
Now I could own my boat, *Tee Kay*, the gillnetter
The snug and round one, warm as a woman
With her stove stoked at night and her lanterns lit
And anchor cast, brooding upon the water
Settled to sleep in the lap of the Skeena.

Now after thirty years, come from an island
To make a home near water: first on a sailing vessel
Towed, each season, to the fishing grounds:
Then the small gasboat, the gillnetter, that belonged
Not to the man who fished, but to the cannery.

Now after thirty years a free man, naturalized,
A man who owned his boat! I smelt the wind
Wetting my face, waves dashing against the *Tee Kay*'s
    sides
The grey dawn opening like a book
At the horizon's rim. I was my own master —
Must prove it now, today! Stooping over the engine
Priming the starter, opening the gas valve,
I felt her throbbing in answer; I laughed
And grasped the fly wheel, swung her over.
She churned off up the river — my own boat, my home.

That was before Pearl Harbor: before a December day
Spent on a restless sea; then anchor in the dusk
And down to bunk to have a bowl of rice.
By lantern light I turned the battery set
To hear brief messages from fishermen
From boat to shore, to learn the weather forecast.
Must have been dozing when I woke up sharp —
What was he saying? Some kind of government order?
"All fishing craft on the high seas must head at once
To the nearest port, report to authorities."
Did they not want our fish, the precious oil?
"No," said the voice, "Our boats were to be examined, searched
For hidden guns, for maps, for treachery. . . ."
I heard, but could not understand. Obeyed,
But as a blind man. The numb fear about my boat,
Tee Kay, found no release in port, off shore,
Rubbing against a fleet of trollers, frail gillnetters
All heading down for Inverness and Tusk
All in the dark, with rumour flying fast.
No one knew more than his fear whispered,
No one explained.
We thought: perhaps it's all a mistake
Perhaps they'll line us up and do a search
Then leave us free for Skeena, Ucluelet —
The time is ripe, the season's fish are running.

74

There was no mistake. It wasn't a joke:
At every fishing port more boats fell in.
Some had no wood, no gasoline; and some
Barely a day's store of food aboard.
So we waited at the Inlet's mouth, till the 16th.

How speak about the long trip south, the last
We ever made, in the last of our boats?
The time my life turned over, love went under
Into the cold unruly sea. Those waves
Washing the cabin's walls
Lashed hate in me.

We left Rupert in two long lines of sixty boats
Strung to the seiners, met and tugged
By *Starpoint* and the naval escort, the corvette.
All day we watched the gloomy sea roughed up
By westerlies, but had to tough it out
Glued to the wheel, weary for sleep, till 2 a.m.

Then, at Lowe Inlet, had brief anchorage.
At Milbanke Sound we ran into heavier seas
The buffeted boats like so many bobbing corks
Strung on a thin rope line that over and over
Would break, be mended by the corvette's men
And then again be snapped by snarling sea.

Day merged into night and day again
Found us with six boats broken loose; some torn
And others gashed with bumping in the dark —
If some drugged fisherman fell off to sleep
And left craft pilotless,
Smashing like blind birds through a log-strewn sea.
Some boats that had no gasoline to keep
Heart thumping in their engines, these
Were plucked aloft in fistfuls by the waves
Then brought down with a thud —
Propellers spinning helpless in mid-air.

So we proceeded into colder, rougher seas,
Seasick and sore, nodding at the wheel,
Then stamping up and down to keep the winter out.

Christmas at sea. The bitterest for me
That any year had given. Even so
Some had a celebration, pooled their funds
And bought the only chicken left in Alert Bay.
Others boiled cabbages in salt sea water,
Pulled out the playing cards and shrugged, and laughed.
As we set sail at midnight, now a thousand boats
Chained to the naval escort, steadily south
Into familiar waters where the forests cooled their feet
At rocks'-end, mountains swam in mist —
As we set sail for home, the young ones, born here, swore
Not softly, into the hissing night. The old men wept.

The rest takes little telling. On the fifteenth night
We passed Point Grey's low hulk, our long line wavered
        shoreward.
Dirty and hungry, sleep lying like a stone
Stuck in our heads, we nosed our broken craft
Into the wharf at Steveston, "Little Tokyo".
The crowd on the dock was silent. Women finding their men
Clung to them searchingly, saying never a word,
Leading them home to the *ofuro** and supper.
Others of us, like me, who knew no one,
Who had no place near the city's centre
Stood lonely on the wharf, holding the *Tee Kay*'s line
For the last time, watching the naval men
Make a note of her number, take my name.
That was the end of my thirty years at the fishing
And the end of my boat, my home.

ANNOUNCER:
These their children, the Niseis, ** were born

*Ofuro—the bath.
**Niseis—generation born in Canada.

Into the new world, called British Columbia home,
Spoke of her as mother, and beheld
Their future in her pungent evergreen.

A YOUNG NISEI:
We lived unto ourselves
Thinking so to be free
Locked in the harbour
Of father and mother
The children incoming
The tide inflowing.

Sometimes at remote midnight
With a burnt-out moon
An orange eye on the river
Or rising before dawn
From a house heavy with sleepers
The man touching my arm
Guiding my hand through the dark
To the boat softly bumping and sucking
Against the wharf;
We go out toward misty islands
Of fog over the river
Jockeying for position;
Till morning steals over, sleepy,
And over our boat's side, leaning
The word comes, Set the nets!
Hiding the unannounced prayer
Resounding in the heart's corners:
May we have a high boat
And the silver salmon leaping!

We lived unto ourselves
Locked in the harbour

I remember the schoolhouse, its battered doorway
The helter-skelter of screaming children
Where the old ones went, my sisters

Soberly with books strapped over their shoulders:
Deliberately bent on learning —

(And learned, soon enough, of
The colour of their skin, and why
Their hair would never turn golden.)

But before the bell rang
For me
My turn at becoming
Before the bell rang
I was out on the hillside
Reaching high over my head for the black ones
The first plump berries of summer;
A scratch on the arm, maybe, a tumble
But filling my pail and singing my song
With the bees humming
And the sun burning.

Then no bell rang for me;
Only the siren.
Only the women crying and the men running.
Only the Mounties writing our names
In the big book; the stifled feeling
Of being caught, corralled.
Only the trucks and a scramble to find
A jacket, a ball, for the bundle.

My blackberries spilled
Smeared purple
Over the doorway.
Never again did I go
Blackberry picking on the hillside.
Never again did I know
That iron schoolbell ringing.

The children incoming
The tide inflowing.

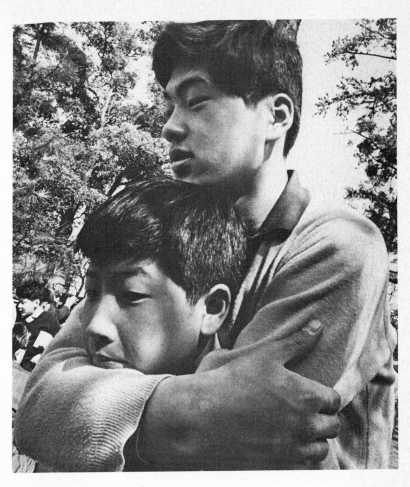

ANNOUNCER:
From the upper islands of the coast
With only one day's notice to depart
Came these, and hundreds like them: Mariko and her
    mother.
In the re-allocation centre, Hastings Park
Mariko writes a letter.

THE LETTER:
I wonder where in the inner country

On what train shooting between two mountains
You fly tonight, Susumu?
When I explain to you how it is here
You will understand, perhaps,
Why I have not been able to tell my mother
About you and me.

It is this: she is continually frightened —
Never having lived so, in a horse stall before.
My bunk is above hers, and all night I lie rigid
For fear to disturb her; but she is disturbed.
She has hung her pink petticoat from my bunk rail
Down over her head, to be private; but nothing is private.
Hundreds of strangers lie breathing around us
Wakeful, or coughing; or in sleep tossing;
Hundreds of strangers pressing upon us
Like horses tethered, tied to a manger.

My mother lies wakeful with her eyes staring.
I cannot see her, but I know. She is thinking:
This is a nightmare. She is back in her home
Embroidering blossoms on a silk kimono
Talking to me of Yosh (the boy I mentioned,
The one I grew up with). She is making plans
To visit the go-between; to bake for a wedding.

My mother cannot believe her dream is over,
That she lies in a manger with her hands tethered.
So you will understand now, Susumu:
I have not been able to tell my mother.
It is hard for me to believe, myself,
How you said the words, how you spoke of a garden
Where my name, MARIKO, would be written in
      flowers. . . .
I wonder where in the inner country
On what train far from this animal silence
This thick night stifling my heart, my nostrils —
Where like a rocket shooting between two planets
Have you flown, Susumu? Have you gone?

ANNOUNCER:
Between the fury and the fear
The window-breaking rabble and the politician's
        blackout,
(Wartime panic fed
On peacetime provocations)
Between the curfew rung
On Powell Street
And the rows of bunks in a public stable
Between the line-ups and the labels and the presentation
        of a one-way ticket
Between these, and the human heart —
There was in every centre one man, a white man —
A minister, a layman — a mayor.

THE MAYOR:
That year the snow came early, lay lightly on our hills
Cooling their colours, pointing up the evergreen
Scribbled over the ledges; at valley's end
Snow muffled with its mantle the gaunt shape,
The smokeless chimney of the copper smelter.

I stood on the station platform reading the message
Telegraphed from Vancouver: "The first contingent,
Sixty-eight persons, arriving on the night train."
Then I looked down our narrow, funnelled valley
My ghost-town village, with hotels closed up
Since gold-rush days; post office perched
Upon a down-hill lurch, leaning towards empty stores.

Sixty-eight persons, and where could they find a pillow?
The government shacks were only half completed,
Without heat or water; there remained a hotel
Half boarded up; a church; some vacant houses
Left tenantless, standing on back streets.
These I tried first; but the neighbours protested:
They had read the newspapers, they did not want
Criminals and spies settling upon their doorsteps.
There was nothing for it but to open the creaking door,

Put stoves and straw in the Golden Gate Hotel.

At seven-fifteen the evening train pulled in.
I stood alone on the platform, waiting.
Slowly the aliens descended, in huddled groups,
Mothers and crying children; boys and girls
Holding a bundle of blankets, cardboard boxes,
A basket of pots and pans, a child's go-cart —
Looking bewildered up and down the platform,
The valley closing in, the hostile village. . . .

I stepped forward, urged into sudden action.
The women cowered, fell back, cried words
In panic to the old men standing surly, helpless.
I collared a young kid, bright, with his eyes snapping:
"You there, you speak English?" "Why, yah! You bet."
We eyed each other, and I smiled. "You see,"
I said, "I'm mayor here . . . your mayor.
This is your home. Can you tell the people that?
Tell them I'm here to meet them, get acquainted,
Find a place for them to sleep." The boy
Nodded. "Okay, I'll tell my mother, sure.
The rest will believe whatever she says to do."

Their conference began. I waited, tense;
Then plunged into the job of lifting crates
And scanty furnishings, getting local lads
To pile it up on trucks; until I felt
A timid touch upon my arm; I turned
And saw the Issei mother.

                              Putting out my hand
I felt hers move, rest for a moment in mine —
Then we were free. We began to work together.

I remember the long looks of my neighbours
As I strode down the street the next morning
Arm in arm with a flock of Japanese kids.
I took them into the store, the post-office,

82

Showed them the ropes, then headed for the school,
If no one else in the town would say "hello"
There was one who would! I knew her
Inside out, like a book — the Principal.

In an hour's time she had them behind desks
Those six, of high school age, those slant-eyed
Black-haired, half-terrified children.
Then I went out to find some carpenters
To build a village in a single day. . . .
It was cold. Light snow covered the hills.
By spring, I vowed, those people would be mine!
This village would be home.

ANNOUNCER:
These were the fathers, mothers, those
Who had to choose another home, another way.
What would they choose? The questioner
Paused with his pencil lifted; gave them a day
To talk together, choose.

THE WIFE:
Either to be a ghost in mountain towns
Abandoned by the fabulous, the seekers
After gold, upon whose bones the forest and the rock
Had feasted; there to sit
With idle hands embroidering the past
Upon a window pane, fed on foreign food
And crowded together in government huts
The men torn from our arms, the family parted,
Or to face the longer, stranger journey
Over the mountain ranges, barred from the sea —
To labour in uncertain soil, inclement weather
Yet labour as one — all the family together?

We looked at each other, you and I, after
So many doubtful years binding our struggles:
Our small plot grown to wider green

Pastured within the Fraser's folds, the shack
Upbuilded to a cottage, now a house —
The cherry trees abloom and strawberry fields
White with the snow of blossom, of promise.
Had it all to be done again, worked at again
By our gnarled hands, in a harsh new land
Where summer passes like a quick hot breath
And winter holds you chained for half the year?
You took my hands, and said: "It's the children's country.
Let them choose." They chafed for independence
Scenting the air of freedom in far fields.
Therefore we had no choice, but one straight way:
The eastward journey into emptiness,
A prairie place called home.

It was harder than hate. Home was a blueprint only.
We lived in a hen coop perched on a farmer's field
Soaked by the sudden storms, the early rains of April.
Yet there was time for ploughing, time to sow
Beet seed upon the strange black soil in rows
Of half an acre; we saw in neighbouring fields'
Bleak tableland, the stabbing green
Of the young wheat; and heard the sweet
Heart-snaring song of meadow-larks; in grass
Withered and brown saw maps move, empty patches
Purple with crocus underneath our feet.

In summer the sun's beak
Tore at our backs bending over the rows
Endless for thinning; the lumpy soil left callouses
Upon our naked knees; mosquitoes swarmed
In frenzied choruses above our heads
Sapping the neck; until a hot wind seared
The field, drove them away in clouds.

I think we had nearly given up, and wept
And gone for government help, another home —
Until, one evening lull, work done

You leaned upon the poplar gate to watch
A lime green sky rim the mauve twilight
While in the pasture fireflies danced
Like lanterns of Japan on prairie air.
Leaning the other way spoke our new friend
The neighbour from the Ukraine;
Touching your arm, using words more broken
Than yours, like scraps of bread left over.

"See how tomorrow is fine. You work
Hard, same as me. We make good harvest time."
He came from a loved land, too, the mild
Plains of the Dneiper where, in early spring
(He said) the violets hid their sweetness. "This land
Is strange and new. But clean and big
And gentle with the wheat. For children too,
Good growing."
He lifted up his hands, his praise; we heard
Over the quickening fields a fresh wind blowing.

ANNOUNCER:
This one was young, a renegade. He wanted the world
In his two hands. He would not make the choice,
But cast it back in their teeth.

NISEI VOICE:
They can't do this to me, Shig said
(Once a Jap, always a Jap)
Why, I went to school with those kids
Vancouver's my home town.

They can't do this to me, Shig said
(Once a Jap, always a Jap)
I'll spend my life in a road camp
In a freight car bunk in the bush.

They'll get tired of me, Shig said
(Once a Jap, always a Jap)
And some dark night I'll buckle my belt

And hitch-hike to the sea.

The Mounties won't get me, Shig said
(Once a Jap, always a Jap)
I'll say I'm a Chinese, see?
It's the underworld for me.

They picked Shig up on a robbery charge
(Once in jail, always in jail)
There were only a few of us such as he
But he blackened our name
Shut the gates to the sea.

ANNOUNCER:
This one was young; but he wanted the world
For others. A philosopher,
He accepted the blow, Pearl Harbor.
He learned the way of waiting.

THE PHILOSOPHER:
To be alone is grace; to see it clear
Without rancour; to let the past be
And the future become. Rarely to remember
The painful needles turning in the flesh.

(I had looked out of the schoolroom window
And could not see the design, held dear
Of the shaken maples; nor the rain, searing and stinging
The burning rain in the eye.

I could not see, nor hear my name called:
Tatsuo, the Pythagoras theorem!
I could not think till the ruler rapped
On the desk, and my mind snapped.

The schoolroom faded, I could not hold
A book again in my hand.
It was the not knowing; the must be gone
Yet the continual fear of going.

Yes, to remember is to go back; to take
The path along the dyke, the lands of my uncle
Stretching away from the river —
The dykeside where we played

Under his fruit trees, canopied with apples,
Falling asleep under a hedgerow of roses
To the gull's shrill chatter and the tide's recurrent
Whisper in the marshland that was home. . . .)

So must I remember. It cannot be hid
Nor hurried from. As long as there abides
No bitterness; only the lesson learned
And the habit of grace chosen, accepted.

CHORUS OF NISEIS:
Home, we discover, is where life is:
Not Manitoba's wheat
Ontario's walled cities
Nor a B.C. fishing fleet.

Home is something more than harbour —
Than father, mother, sons;
Home is the white face leaning over your shoulder
As well as the darker ones.

Home is labour, with the hand and heart,
The hard doing, and the rest when done;
A wider sea than we knew, a deeper earth,
A more enduring sun.

WHAT DO I REMEMBER OF THE EVACUATION?

Joy Kogawa

What do I remember of the evacuation?
I remember my father telling Tim and me
About the mountains and the train
And the excitement of going on a trip.
What do I remember of the evacuation?
I remember my mother wrapping
A blanket around me and my
Pretending to fall asleep so she would be happy
Though I was so excited I couldn't sleep
(I hear there were people herded
Into the Hastings Park like cattle.
Families were made to move in two hours
Abandoning everything, leaving pets
And possessions at gun point.
I hear families were broken up
Men were forced to work. I heard
It whispered late at night
That there was suffering) and
I missed my dolls.
What do I remember of the evacuation?
I remember Miss Foster and Miss Tucker
Who still live in Vancouver
And who did what they could
And loved the children and who gave me
A puzzle to play with on the train.
And I remember the mountains and I was
Six years old and I swear I saw a giant
Gulliver of Gulliver's Travels scanning the horizon
And when I told my mother she believed it too
And I remember how careful my parents were
Not to bruise us with bitterness
And I remember the puzzle of Lorraine Life
Who said "Don't insult me" when I
Proudly wrote my name in Japanese
And Tim flew the Union Jack

When the war was over but Lorraine
And her friends spat on us anyway
And I prayed to the God who loves
All the children in his sight
That I might be white.

THE TRENCH DWELLERS
Jack Hodgins

Macken this, Macken that. Gerry Mack had had enough. Why should he waste his life riding ferries to weddings and family reunions? There were already too many things you were forced to do in this world whether you liked them or not. "And I've hated those family gatherings," he said, "for as long as I can remember. Why else would I move away?"

The problem was that Gerry's Aunt Nora Macken really did believe family was important. She used to tell how the Mackens first settled on the north slope of the valley more than fifty years ago when Black Alex her father brought the whole dozen of his children onto the Island in his touring car and started hacking a farm out of what had for centuries been pure timber land. And would tell, too, that by now there was hardly a household left in all the valley that wasn't related to them in one way or another. What Aunt Nora called The Immediate Family had grown to include more than four hundred people, three-quarters of whom were named Smith or O'Brien or Laitenen though she called them all the Mackens.

There wasn't any real substitute for having a lot of relatives, she said. And the people who knew her best, this tall big-footed old maid living out on that useless farm, said that yes, she was right, there was no substitute for family.

And because Nora Macken lived on those three hundred acres of farmland which had gone back already in two generations to second-growth timber, she thought it her duty every time there was a wedding or a funeral to call a reunion of The Immediate Family the day after the ceremony. More than three hundred relatives gathered. The older people, her own generation, spent the day in the house telling each other stories about Black Alex, reassuring one another that he really was as mean and miserable as they remembered but that it couldn't be denied he was a bit of a character too all the same.

The young adults drank beer outside in the grassy yard or on the verandah and talked about their jobs and their houses and tried to find out how much money each other was earning. The children chased each other between the dead orchard trees and climbed the rickety ladders to the barn mow and fought over the sticky slices of cake Nora Macken put outside on a folding card table in the sun.

As for someone like Gerry Mack, her nephew, who was the only member of The Immediate Family ever to move off Vancouver Island, these events were more than he could bear.

When Gerry was twenty years old he very nearly married Karen O'Brien, a pretty blonde he'd gone all the way through school with. They went to movies together on Saturday nights and sometimes to dances, and afterwards they parked up the gravel road to the city dump to kiss each other until their mouths were raw. But Karen was already a member of The Immediate Family and had half a dozen brothers eager to increase the population. Gerry balked at marriage. He was the son of one of Nora's older brothers and had wished since the time he was six years old that he'd been an orphan.

Soon after dumping Karen O'Brien he met a stoop-shouldered secretary named April Klamp, who was plain-looking and very dull and wore clothes that looked as if they were bought for someone else, perhaps her mother. But she was an only child and had no relatives at all, only a pair of doddering parents who didn't care very much what happened to her. Gerry asked her to marry him a week after their first meeting and of course she accepted. No one before had even given her so much as a second look.

Some members of The Immediate Family had a few words to say about it. It seemed odd, they said, that a young man as vibrant as Gerry couldn't find himself a wife who was more of a match. Aunt Nora, too, thought it was unusual, but she'd given Gerry up long ago as not a real Macken at heart. And besides, she said, it could have been worse. He could have married a churchgoer (something no Macken had ever done) or worse still remained a bachelor (something three of her brothers had done and become cranky old grouches as a result). "Just watch him," she said. "He'll cut off his nose to spite his face."

Gerry didn't particularly care what any of them thought.

Before his wedding he took two letters off his name and became Gerry Mack. He got no argument from April, of course. She was quick to agree that having too much family was worse than having none at all. She didn't even mind that he insisted on getting married seventy miles down-island by a minister she'd never met so that it would be impossible to have a reception afterwards. And when he told her they would live on the mainland she merely nodded and said it was about time one of the Mackens showed a little spunk. Personally, she said, she'd always hated living on an island. She agreed with everything that Gerry Mack said and never took her eyes off his face while he spoke. It was clear to everyone that when Gerry married her what he got was not a separate person to live with but an extension of himself. Aunt Nora said he could have gone out and bought a wooden leg if that was all he wanted.

Though she added, "At least they won't ever get into a fight. An extra limb doesn't talk back."

Their intention was to move far inland but Gerry hadn't driven a hundred miles up the Fraser Valley before he realized he couldn't stand to be away from the coast. They turned back and settled in a little town on the edge of the strait, facing across to the Island, directly across to the valley where he had grown up. They bought a house fifty feet from the beach, with huge plate glass windows facing west, and began saving their money to buy a small boat of their own so they could fish in the evenings.

Because he was a young man with a good rich voice and many opinions, Gerry had no trouble getting a job as an open-line moderator for the new radio station. He spent the first week voicing as many outlandish ideas as he could think of and being as rude as he dared to people who phoned in, so it didn't take long for him to draw most listeners away from the competing station. Within a month he had a large and faithful following on both sides of the strait. People didn't say they listened to CLCB, they said they listened to Gerry Mack's station.

What pleased him most was knowing that whether they liked it or not, most of The Immediate Family would be listening to him every day. He could imagine them in their houses, cringing whenever he was rude to callers, and hoping no one else realized where he'd come from, and saying Thank goodness he'd had the sense to change his name. He made a habit of saying "So long Nora" every day as a sign-off but didn't tell anyone what it meant. People in the mainland town guessed that Nora must have been his wife's middle name or else the name of a grandmother who'd died when he was a little boy. None of them ever guessed of course that Aunt Nora Macken over on the Island sat by her radio every morning for the whole time he was on and went red in the face when he signed off, and told herself maybe he was the only real Macken in the lot after all, though she could spank him for his cheek.

And that, he thought, will show you that here's one Macken who has no need for family.

Though he did not know then, of course, that even the most weak-minded and agreeable wife could suddenly find a backbone and will in herself when she became pregnant. He was sitting in the living room with his feet up on the walnut coffee table looking for good controversial topics in the newspaper when she handed him the wedding invitation that had arrived in the mail that morning. "I think we should go," she said.

"The hell you say," he said, and read through the silver script. "We hardly know them. Who's this Peter O'Brien to us?"

"A cousin," she said. "But that doesn't matter. I think we should be there for the reunion the next day."

Gerry put down the newspaper and looked at his wife. She was rubbing a hand over her round swollen belly. "What for?" he said. "I've been to a million of them. They're all the same. I thought we moved over here to get away from all that."

She sat down beside him on the sofa and put her head against his shoulder. "It's been a year since we've even put a foot on the Island. Let's go just for the fun."

He looked down into her plain mousey hair, her white scalp. She had never asked for a thing before. "We'll go," he said, "but only on the condition that we leave the minute I can't stand any more."

They took the two-hour ferry ride across the strait, and though he sat with a book in his lap and tried to read he found it hard to concentrate and spent a lot of time watching the Island get closer and bigger and more distinct. He hated sitting idle, he was a man who liked to be doing things, and right now he would have preferred to be at work in the radio station or digging in his garden.

Aunt Nora outdid herself. "Lord," she said. "This must be the best reunion ever. There are three hundred and fifty people here, at least, and listen to that racket! When the Mackens get together there's no such thing as a lull in the conversation, there's never a moment when tongues have ceased."

"They do seem to have the gift of the gab," April said.

"A Macken," Aunt Nora said, smiling, "is a sociable person. A Macken enjoys company and conversation."

Macken this Macken that, Gerry thought.

His cousin George Smith put a bottle of beer in his hand and steered him across the yard to lean up against someone's car. He said he couldn't understand why Gerry put up with all the bullshit he had to listen to on his show. He wanted to know why Gerry didn't just threaten to quit his job if people wouldn't smarten up.

Gerry noticed that the whole back yard and orchard were filled with parked cars and that against nearly every car there was at least one pair leaning and drinking beer and talking. Only the old ones were inside. April was standing straighter than he'd ever seen her, laughing with a bunch of women gathered beside a new Buick. "It doesn't matter a damn to me what they say," he told George Smith. "It's just part of my job to listen. Sometimes I tell them to take a flying leap, but what the hell? Who cares?"

George told him he'd cleared over fifteen hundred dollars last month, working in the pulp and paper mill, most of it from overtime. He said he couldn't understand why most of the rest of them worked in the logging camp or in stores in town where there was hardly any overtime at all. It was overtime, he said, that made it possible for him to buy this here little baby they were leaning on. He pushed down on the front fender of the sports car and rocked it gently and with great fondness. Then he asked Gerry if a person working for a radio station got paid a salary or a wage, and what kind of car was he driving anyways? Gerry pointed vaguely across the yard and said as far as he was concerned it was just a way of getting places. But George told him if he got enough overtime in the next few months he intended to buy himself a truck and camper so he could take more weekends off to go fishing up in the lakes. "Everybody's got one," he said. "One time I went up to Gooseneck Lake with Jim and Harriet and there were sixteen truck-and-campers there already. Nine of them were Mackens. Even old Uncle Morris was there, driving a brand new Chev, and he only makes the minimum wage at *his* job. I told him, I said How could you afford a thing like that? and he said It pays to have a son in the car-selling business. The bastard. I said I bet you'll be paying for that god damn thing for the rest of your life."

"And he said?" Gerry said.

"Nothing," George said. "He just told me I was jealous. Ha!"

April came across the yard and led Gerry away towards a large group of people sitting in lawn chairs in a circle and doing a lot of laughing. But Aunt Nora, tall Aunt Nora with all her dyed-black hair piled up on top of her head, intercepted them and took them inside so that Uncle Morgan, who had been sick in the hospital the whole time they were engaged, could meet April. "It won't do," she said, "to have strangers in the same family." She pushed them right into her cluttered little living room and made someone get up so April could have a comfortable chair. Gerry leaned against the door frame and wondered if old Black Alex realized when he was alive that the dozen kids he'd hauled onto the Island in his touring car would eventually become these aging wrinkled people.

And of course it was Black Alex they were talking about. Uncle Morris said, "I mind the time he said to me Get off that roof boy or I'll stuff you down the chimney!" He laughed so hard at that he had to haul out a handkerchief to wipe the tears off his big red face.

Aunt Nora, too, shrieked. "Oh, that was his favourite! He was always threatening to stuff one of us down the chimney." Though she was careful to explain to April that never in his life did he do any such thing to any of them, that in fact the worst he ever did was apply the toe of his boot to their backsides. "He was a noisy man," she said, "but some of us learned how to handle him."

Then she drew everybody's attention to April and said, "As you can easily see, there's one more little Macken waiting to be born. Boy or girl we wish it luck."

"D'you know?" Uncle Morgan said. "Not one person in the family has ever named a child after Dad."

"No wonder!" Aunt Nora cried. "There could only be one Alex Macken. No one else would dare try to match him."

"Or want to," Aunt Katherine said. "Suppose they got his temper too, along with his name."

"One thing for sure," Aunt Nora said. "He'll have plenty of cousins to play with. He'll never run out of playmates or friends." Then, remembering, she added, "Of course, as long as they keep him isolated over there on the mainland I suppose he'll miss out on everything."

"It's terrible having no one to play with," April said. "Especially if you're too shy to go out making friends on your own. Just ask me, I know. At least with cousins you don't have to start from scratch. Nobody needs to be scared of a relative."

"Right!" Aunt Nora said, and looked right at Gerry. "Though there are some people who think loneliness is a prize to be sought after."

Gerry Mack knew, of course, that something had happened

to the wife he thought was a sure bet to remain constant. It came as something of a surprise. After all, who expected an adult's foot to suddenly turn into a hand or start growing off in a new direction? He brooded about it all the way home on the ferry and wouldn't speak to her even while she got ready for bed. He sat in his living room until he was sure she'd gone to sleep, then he tiptoed into the bedroom and undressed without turning on the light.

The next day he held off the phone calls that came into the station and kept the air waves to himself. From his little sound-booth he could look out across the strait. "From over here," he told his listeners, "from here on the mainland, Vancouver Island is just a pale blue chain of mountains stretched right across your whole range of vision. A jagged-backed wall between us and the open sea. Go have a look. Stop what you're doing for a minute and go to your window." He waited for a while, and thought not of the housewives who were moving to the ocean side of their houses, but of the islanders who were over there listening and wondering what he was up to.

"There it is," he said. "Twenty miles away. I bet you hardly ever notice it there, like a fence that borders the back yard." He drank a mouthful of the coffee he kept with him throughout the show. "Now those of you who've been across on the ferry know that as you get closer those mountains begin to take on shapes and change from blue to green and show big chunks of logged-off sections and zig-zag logging roads like knife-scars up their sides. And closer still, of course, you see that along the edge of the Island, stretched out along the shelf of flatter land, is a chain of farms and fishing villages and towns and tourist resorts and bays full of log booms and peninsulas dotted with summer cabins. All of it, ladies and gentlemen, facing over to us as if those people too think those mountains are nothing but a wall at their backs, holding off the Pacific."

He gulped coffee again and glanced at his watch. He thought of the mainlanders looking across. He thought of the islanders wondering what the hell he was talking about. Then he said, "But the funny thing is this: to those people over there on that island this mainland they spend most of their lives facing is nothing but a blue chain of jagged mountains stretched across their vision like a wall separating them from the rest of North America. That continent behind us doesn't even exist for some of them. To them we look just the same as they do to us."

Then, just before opening the telephone lines to callers, he said, "What we live in is a trench. Do you suppose trench-dwellers think any different from the rest of the world?"

His line was busy for the rest of the morning. Most wanted to talk about why they liked living in a place like this, some asked him couldn't he think of a more pleasant comparison to make, and a few tried to change the subject to the recent tax increase. One long-distance call came in from the Island, an old man who told him he was jabbering nonsense and ought to be locked up, some place where all he could see would be bars and padded walls. "If you want to live in a trench," he said, "I'll dig you one. Six feet long by six feet deep." Gerry Mack hung up on his cackling laughter and vowed he would never cross that strait again.

But April told him that didn't mean *she* couldn't go across just whenever she felt like it.

So that when the next wedding invitation arrived he was ready for her announcement. Even if he didn't want to go, she said, she was heading across and taking Jimmy with her. He couldn't deprive her forever of the pleasure of showing off her son to his family. And Jimmy, too, had a right to meet his cousins. She was pregnant again and there was a new hard glint in her eye. Gerry Mack, when she talked like that to him, felt very old and wondered what life would have been like if he'd married Karen O'Brien. If that's what happened to women, he thought, you might as well marry your own sister.

When she came back she told him the reunion of course was a huge success and everybody asked where he was. She'd stayed right at Aunt Nora's, she said, and it was amazing how much room there was in that old farm house when everyone else had gone home. She'd felt right at home there. Jimmy had had a wonderful time, had made friends with hundreds of cousins, and could hardly wait for the next time they went over. And oh yes, Aunt Nora sent him a message.

"What is it?" he said, weary.

"She says there's a wonderful new man on *their* radio station. She says she doesn't know of a single Macken who still listens to you. This new fellow plays softer music and isn't nearly so rude to his callers. She says people do appreciate good manners after all and she can't think of one good reason for you not to be at the next wedding."

"At the rate they're marrying," he said, "The Immediate Family will soon swallow up the whole Island."

"The Mackens believe in marriage," she said. "And in sticking together."

Mackens this Mackens that, Gerry Mack thought.

"Nora told me her father used to say being a Macken was like being part of a club. Or a religion."

"Do you know why they call him Black Alex?"

"Why?"

"When he was alive people used to call him Nigger Alex because his hair was so black and you never saw him without dirt on his hands and face. People on the Island never saw a real black man in those days. But the 'children' decided after his death that Black Alex was politer and what people would've called him if they'd only stopped to think."

"Well at least they called him something," she said. "It shows he was liked. It shows people noticed him. I never heard anyone call you anything but Gerry, an insipid name if I ever heard one. Pretty soon those people over there will forget you even exist."

"That's fine with me," Gerry Mack said, and went outside to sprinkle powder on his rose leaves.

But she followed him. "Sometimes I don't think it's family you're trying to get away from at all. I think it's humanity itself."

"Don't be ridiculous," he said. "If that was what I wanted I'd

99

have become a hermit."

"What else are we?" She was on the verge of tears. "You don't let Jimmy play with anyone else's kids, none of them are good enough for you. And we've hardly any friends ourselves."

"Don't harp," he said. "Don't nag at me."

It passed through his mind to tell her she had no business going against his wishes when it came to bringing up the boy. But he was a strange kid anyway, and Gerry had always been uncomfortable with children. It was easier to let her do what she wanted with him.

When April went across to George Smith's wedding (his second) and took Jimmy and the baby with her he knew she would not be coming back. He wasn't surprised when she didn't get off the Sunday evening ferry. He didn't even bother watching the ferries coming in during the next week. The only surprise was the sight of Aunt Nora getting out of a taxi the following weekend and throwing herself into the leather armchair in Gerry's living room.

"My God," she said. "It looks as if you could walk across in fifteen minutes but that ferry takes forever."

"Where's April?" he said.

The wedding, she told him, was lovely. Because it was George's second the girl didn't try to make it into too much of a thing but just as many people turned out for it as for his first. "He's got a real dandy this time," she said. "He's not going to want to spend so much time at his precious pulp mill when he's got this one waiting at home. She's got outdoor teeth of course, but still she's darned pretty!"

Gerry said George's first wife hadn't been much to look at but then George was no prize himself.

Then, suddenly, Aunt Nora said, "I think she'll be asking you for a legal separation."

"Who?" he said, stupidly.

"I told her she could live with me. There's too much room in that old house for one person. I'll enjoy the company. I remember Dad saying if a Macken couldn't count on one of his own relatives in times of trouble, who could he count on? That little boy of yours is going to look just like him." She stood up and took off her coat and laid it over the back of her chair. Then she took a cigarette out of her purse and lit it and sat down again.

"If you want to come back with me and try to patch it up, that's all right."

"Patch what up?" he said. "We haven't even had a fight."

But she acted as if she hadn't heard. "I'll tell you something, Gerry, you've got spunk. Maybe you're the only real Macken in the whole kaboodle."

"Ha."

"And if you and April patch it up, if you want to live on the farm, that's all right with me too."

"Why should I want to live there?"

"It's the family homestead," she said, as if it was something he might have forgotten. "It's where your grandfather started out. Where the family began."

Gerry grunted and went to the refrigerator to get himself a bottle of beer.

"Well somebody will have to take it over some day," she said. "You can see what's happened to the farm with just an old maid living on it. He never should have left it to me in the first place. Except, of course, it's the best place for holding family get-togethers and I know if it was left to anyone else they'd never get done."

"Look," he said. "You got her and my two kids. Three for one. That sounds like a pretty good trade to me."

"I just can't believe you don't care about those children," Aunt Nora said. "Those two little boys. No Macken has ever abandoned his own children. It doesn't seem natural."

"Natural," Gerry Mack said, and tilted up his bottle of beer.

But when she caught the morning ferry home he did not go with her. In fact, he was to make only one more visit to the Island, and that would not be until two years later when he attended his son's funeral. Aunt Nora phoned him in the middle of the day to say the boy had drowned in a swimming accident. The Immediate Family was at the funeral, four hundred or so of them, standing all over the graveyard where Mackens were buried. He'd sat beside April in the chapel but when they got to the graveside she seemed to be surrounded by relatives and he was left alone, on the far side of the ugly hole they were putting his son in. Aunts and cousins were weeping openly but April in their midst stared straight ahead with her jaw set like stone. She appeared then to have lost all of the slump that was once in her back. Even her mousey brown hair seemed to have taken on more life. When their eyes met she nodded in a way that might have been saying "Thank you" or might have been only a dismissal, or could perhaps have been simply acknowledging she had noticed his, a stranger's, presence.

Aunt Nora, afterwards, cornered him in her little living room. She seemed smaller now, slightly stooped, getting old. There were deep lines in her face. "Now," she said. "Now do you see where your place is? Now do you see where you belong?"

He turned, tried to find someone to rescue him.

"This whole farm, Gerry, it's yours. Just move here, stay here where you belong."

And it was April who rescued him after all. She came into the room swiftly, her eyes darting with the quick concern of a hostess making sure everything was going well. "Oh Nora!" she said. "Uncle Morris was asking for you. I promised I'd take you to him."

When the old woman stood up to leave, April let her gaze flicker momentarily over him. Her complexion against the black dress looked nearly ivory. Beautiful skin. She would be a beautiful woman yet. "George Smith was wondering where you were," she said. "I told him I thought you'd already gone home."

For several years after that Aunt Nora visited the mainland

102

every summer to report to Gerry on his wife and remaining son and to tell him all about the weddings and reunions he'd missed. April, she told him, had taken over the last reunion completely, did all the planning and most of the work. And some people on the Island were listening to him again she said, now that he was only reading the news, once a day.

But she stopped coming altogether years later when he sold the seaside house and moved in with a woman far up a gravel road behind town, in a junky unpainted house beside a swamp. She had nearly a dozen children from various fathers, some Scandinavian, two Indian, and one Chinese, and her name was Netty Conroy. Which meant, Aunt Nora Macken was soon able to discover after a little investigation, that she was related to more than half the people who lived in that mainland town, not to mention most who lived in the countryside around it. It was a strange thing, she told The Immediate Family, but she still felt closer to Gerry Mack than to any of the rest of them. Perhaps it was because she, too, had had a tendency to cut off her nose to spite her face. Everyone laughed at the notion because of course, they said, Aunt Nora had always had everything just the way she wanted it in this world.

NO LONGER
Chief Dan George

No longer
  can I give you a handful of berries as a gift,
no longer
  are the roots I dig used as medicine,
no longer
  can I sing a song to please the salmon,
no longer
  does the pipe I smoke make others sit
  with me in friendship,
no longer
  does anyone want to walk with me to the
  blue mountains to pray,
no longer
  does the deer trust my footsteps . . .

INDIAN CHILDREN
Thelma Reid Lower

Indian children stand by the highways
Like sunflowers, turning their heads.
They do not follow the golden sun.
They watch the great white scheme
Rolling by, on wheels.

A NON-ROMANCE IN THE MOOSE COUNTRY
Paul St. Pierre

Anahim Lake — This is the story of the big-game guide and the lawyer's wife. They did not marry. It is not a romance. Rather, it is a highly moral tale — one which will, I am sure, make better husbands and fathers of us all — females excepted, of course. The guide now speaks:

She was a customer that I will always remember. Always. She was a woman who made a very deep impression on me.

Her husband was a lawyer in the United States. She had left him down there and come up to hunt moose on her own. He was not with her. As I say, she left him down in the States. I guess that country could scarcely have operated with both of them away at the same time.

She talked lots about him, though. I felt just as if I knew him. His character was made very clear to me. Extremely clear. Absolutely clear. He knew all about how the United States ought to be run and she knew all about how my guiding business ought to be run. They must have made quite a pair.

We set out into the mountains with four pack horses. I was glad to have those pack horses along, quite apart from the way they so kindly helped us pack our gear into the hills. They were listeners, those pack horses, and she was a woman who needed a good listener — at all times.

In the morning, she would start talking, a steady regular flow of words that never dried up until sundown. When she got up in the morning, it was just as if you had set the arm of a gramophone that never ran down. I felt that there was five of us to listen, myself and the four horses.

And I am proud to say that those horses all took up their share. There was not a slacker among them. For a fifth of the time I listened to her. Then I would look one of the pack horses in the eye. I would not say anything to that horse, I would just look at him. And he would know that it was his turn to listen. After a little time, he would kick the horse behind, or pass the message along in some other way, and that horse would take over the chore of listening to her explain how her husband the lawyer felt about the Supreme Court.

On the first day out, we did not have too much time to hunt moose or even to look at the scenery. From time to time I would point out to her the pretty colors on the poplars or the nice, clear, quiet looks of the mountains. But she would usually just say "Yes, yes," and then continue to talk about whatever it was that I didn't want to understand. The second day, she developed a thirst about mid-day. I was not surprised.

"I must have some fresh water to drink," she said.

"There is some water there."

"No," she said, "that water is stagnant."

A mile or two later, I found her some more water. No, she said, that water was not fit for human consumption. Every time I found water for her, it was unsatisfactory water. I never realized before that I had been poisoning myself in this country for forty-seven years. Finally, we came to a little creek.

"There is running water," she said. "That is the kind of water to drink." Personally, I had never drunk from that creek, because it flows out of an alkali flat. I started to explain this to her, but she got off her saddle horse saying that this was good clear water and what a pity it was that I had been so long in finding it.

She remained very active all that night, stumbling over me in my bed roll as she wandered around the camp, talking about her indigestion. Next morning she said she had decided that it was the bacon that did it. I said yes, I figured it was the bacon.

We saw a number of cow moose, but cows were out of season then. She did not approve of that. She explained to me why a bull moose season was very bad game management. She went into a lot of detail on that subject. I have not retained all of what she told me. All I remember is the basic principle that you gun down every cow and calf you can find in order to build up a herd.

Anyway, to everything she said, I would always say "You may well be right." Then if she pushed me, I would say "Yes, indeed, you may well be right." This was usually all she required.

I think maybe that was the way her husband the lawyer talked to her also. He had neglected to send me written instructions when he sent his woman to me, but that was all right. I hit on the formula independently. We had both struck it on our own, so to speak. Anything she said, I said "You may well be right."

On the way out, we spotted a young bull moose. "I think that is a bull," I said.

But she knew all about moose. "That is a cow," she said. "It has no horns."

"You may well be right," I said, and we rode on. When we got back to camp she said that it had been a very unsatisfactory hunt. I agreed with her on that, too.

DREAM HORSES, PLATEAU NORTH
Allan Safarik

In the hard bloody night
horses hobbled to the echo
of brass tearshape bells
that jingle and jump like sparks
in dry grass

three horses
on the Bella Coola Road
stand and stare straight
into the headlights
their great brown haunches
some shiny mercurial liquid
poured into a hollow of dark

poured into dull tired eyes
and they turned and reared
stamping the dust
those crippled front legs
blackened sticks in a fire
twisting the light
stamping the memory
of horses.

Middle of the next day
Young Billyboy
in the Alexis Creek beer parlour
"There's a hole in my glass. Lots
of holes in the glasses in this place."

Young Billyboy
born 1891 Anahim Reserve
"I always sing my own song
when I ride bucking horse. One
time I wake up I hear that song,
you know, my bucking horse song."

"On one bad horse from Chilko Ranch
I win first prize for Big Creek. Yes
that's right, Big Creek. I forget his
name that horse. I make $75 and I'm
pretty happy yet.
I go all the way to Anahim Lake.
I lose my stirrup on the saddle but
I win first prize bareback. I'm pretty
happy too, that time."

"Nine stampede I get
first prize Williams Lake. Nine stampede.
At Williams Lake they tell me,
Billyboy, you good rider. Good rider."

"I quit about nine years ago. Nine
years ago I quit. At Anahim I didn't
let go of rope. I get hurt, my hand.
I quit."

ELEPHANTS
Pat Lane

The cracked cedar
bunkhouse hangs behind me like a gray pueblo
in the sundown where I sit
to carve an elephant
from a hunk of brown soap
for the Indian boy
who lives in the village a mile back
in the bush.

The alcoholic truck-driver
and the cat-skinner sit beside
me with their eyes closed —
all of us waiting out the last hour
until we go back on the grade —

and I try to forget the forever
clank   clank   clank
across the grade
pounding stones and earth to powder
for hours in mosquito-darkness
of the endless cold mountain night.

The elephant takes form —
my knife caresses smooth soap
scaling off curls of brown
which the boy saves to take home
to his mother in the village.

Finished, I hand the carving to him
and he looks at the image of the great
beast for a long time
then sets it on dry cedar
and looks up at me:
                    What's an elephant?
he asks me

so I tell him of the elephants
and their jungles — the story
of the elephant graveyard
which no-one has ever found
and how the silent
animals of the rain-forest
go away to die somewhere
in the limberlost of distances
and he smiles at me

tells me of his father's
graveyard where his people have been
buried for years. So far back
no-one remembers when it started
and I ask him where the graveyard is
and he tells me it is gone
now where no-one will ever find it
buried under the grade of the new
highway.

WEST COAST
Frank Davey

Nothing sadder than the picture window
overlooking the sea
and the gulls
        wheeling out
then back to land.

Here on sudden shores
slow lines of covered wagons
lines of laboring steam engines
have ended.
Ended in rows and rows
of sprawling ranch houses
each with its elongated window
looking tiredly away:
the richest
        ironically
by the beach.

Canute would have turned back the sea
but here in the west
amid ocean gray and mist
is denser truth.

QUESTIONS ON THE THEME:
The West Coast Experience

1.   In his introduction to *Stories from Pacific and Arctic Canada* Andreas Schroeder says, "It is a commonplace that artists tend to be glorified cartographers busily compiling maps of where they live and how to get there." Consider how Eric Nicol, Roderick Haig-Brown, Pat Lane, and Paul St. Pierre may be described as cartographers. Consider too how each of these authors does much more than simply make maps.

2.   The selections by bp nichol, Andreas Schroeder, and Susan Goldwater may be described, perhaps, as non-realistic. Consider what this term means. Consider how each of these writers has used metaphor quite literally. For what reason? What is an allegory? Can these selections be seen as saying anything about everyday "reality", or must they be considered as relevant only to their own worlds?

3.   In one way or another the sea finds its way into a good many of these selections. Consider how the image of water is used, perhaps symbolically, by Phyllis Webb, Jack Hodgins, Frank Davey, and Andreas Schroeder. Is there any similarity amongst the authors' attitudes to the sea? Are there important differences? Are the main characters of "The Trench Dwellers" amongst those described in "West Coast"? While Davey and Hodgins treat the ocean as a concrete limited presence with meaning, Schroeder expands its use to abstract, perhaps metaphysical significance. Comment.

4.   What special problems must be considered while writing a radio play? How does Dorothy Livesay keep listener interest in "Call My People Home"? What evidence is there in the text that she was aware of this as a piece of work to be *heard* rather than simply read? If you were rewriting "Encounter with an Archangel" as a radio play, what changes would you make? With the help of friends record "Call My People Home" on tape for the rest of the class. Read passages from other selections too, such as "Images in Place of Logging" or "Elephants". Consider

the importance of sound in poetry. How important is sound in "killer whale"?

5. "The Late Man" has more than once been made into a film. Can you see what aspects of the story would make the conversion fairly simple? What different problems is the maker of a film script faced with compared to the writer of the short story? What advantages does the script writer have? As a group or individual project, consider making a film of one of the selections in this text. Either "Images in Place of Logging" or "I Just Love Dogs" would be ideal for the three-and-a-half-minute Super-8 cartridge. Begin by planning a script carefully, considering both the visual and audio aspects of it. Your teacher will be able to supply you with a book or booklet outlining the process if you feel you need direction.

6. Read a descriptive account of the killer whale in an encyclopedia. Compare the scientific treatment with the poetic treatment given him by bill bissett and Susan Musgrave. In what way do these poets feel similar responses? What are the differences in their treatment of the experience? Can you think of any phenomenon in your immediate surroundings that calls up similar responses in you? What creature could be symbolically equivalent to the killer whale in your part of the country?

7. The west coast, like other parts of the country, is made up of a mosaic of peoples from various backgrounds. Consider what contribution to the west coast scene is being made by the people in "Encounter with an Archangel", "The Trench Dwellers", "Call My People Home", "Elephants", and "Dream Horses, Plateau North".

8. Choose a book from the bibliography to read. Write a paper in which you relate the book to some of the concepts mentioned in the introduction to this text.

9. Make a thorough study of the works of any one west coast writer. Compare his or her relationship to the region with that of a selection of writers found in this anthology.

10. For the selection you enjoyed or admired most, attempt to show how its significance extends beyond a regional concern and has something to say of universal appeal and importance.

BIBLIOGRAPHY

BIOGRAPHICAL INFORMATION

Carl F. Klinck, *A Literary History of Canada: Canadian Literature in English*, University of Toronto Press

Norah Story, *The Oxford Companion to Canadian History and Literature*, Oxford University Press

William Stewart Wallace, *The Macmillan Dictionary of Canadian Biography*, Macmillan of Canada

ANTHOLOGIES

J. Brown (ed.), *West Coast Seen*, Talonbooks

Gary Geddes (ed.), *Skookum Wawa*, Oxford University Press

Andreas Schroeder and Rudy Wiebe (eds.), *Stories from Pacific and Arctic Canada*, Macmillan of Canada

R. Watters (ed.), *British Columbia: A Centennial Anthology*, McClelland & Stewart

J. Michael Yates (ed.), *Contemporary Poetry of British Columbia*, Sono Nis

PLAYS

Cam Hubert, *The Twin Sinks of Alan Sammy*, Playwrights' Co-op

Joan Mason Hurley, *Canadian One-Act Plays for Women*, A Room of One's Own Press

George Ryga, *The Ecstasy of Rita Joe and Other Plays*, Talonbooks

Beverley Simons, *Crabdance*, Talonbooks

NON-FICTION

M. Wylie Blanchet, *The Curve of Time*, Gray's Publishing

Emily Carr, *Klee Wyck*, Clarke, Irwin

George Clutesi, *Potlatch*, Gray's Publishing

Alan Fotheringham, *Collected and Bound*, November House

Chief Dan George and Helmut Hirnschall, *My Heart Soars*, Hancock House

Simma Holt, *Terror in the Name of God*, Crown

Hugh W. McKervill, *The Salmon People*, Gray's Publishing

Eric Nicol, *The Best of Eric Nicol*, Pocket Books

John Norris, *Strangers Entertained*, Evergreen

R. M. Patterson, *Far Pastures,* Gray's Publishing
Ian Smith, *The Unknown Island*, J. J. Douglas
Paul St. Pierre, *Chilcotin Holiday*, McGraw-Hill Ryerson
Takashima, *A Child in a Prison Camp,* Tundra

SHORT STORIES
Collections
George Bowering, *Flycatcher*, Oberon
Michael Bullock, *Green Beginnings, Black Endings*, Sono Nis
George Clutesi, *Son of Raven, Son of Deer*, Gray's Publishing
Jack Hodgins, *Spit Delaney's Island*, Macmillan of Canada
Malcolm Lowry, *Hear Us O Lord from Heaven Thy Dwelling Place*, McClelland & Stewart
George McWhirter, *Bodyworks*, Oberon
Andreas Schroeder, *The Late Man*, Sono Nis
Ethel Wilson, *Mrs. Golightly and Other Stories*, Macmillan of Canada
Single
Gladys Hindmarsh, "How It Feels", in *Stories from Pacific and Arctic Canada*
Anne Marriott, "Institutions", in *Journal of Canadian Fiction* 3:2
Beverley Mitchell, S.S.A., "Letter to Sakaye", in *Stories from Pacific and Arctic Canada*
Marvin Smith, "Adding Up", in *Event* 3:3, and "Fence" in *Event* 3:1

NOVELS
Earle Birney, *Down the Long Table*, McClelland & Stewart
George Bowering, *Mirror on the Floor*, McClelland & Stewart
Alan Fry, *How a People Die*, PaperJacks
M. A. Grainger, *Woodsmen of the West*, McClelland & Stewart
Roderick Haig-Brown, *On the Highest Hill*, Collins
Robert Harlow, *A Gift of Echoes* and *Royal Murdoch*, Macmillan of Canada; *Scann*, Sono Nis
Christie Harris, *Once Upon a Totem*, McClelland & Stewart
Patricia Joudry, *Dweller on the Threshold*, McClelland & Stewart

118

Norman Newton, *The Big Stuffed Hand of Friendship*,
   McClelland & Stewart
George Payerle, *The Afterpeople*, Anansi
Ernest Perrault, *The Kingdom Carver*, Doubleday
Paul St. Pierre, *Breaking Smith's Quarter Horse*, McGraw-Hill
   Ryerson
Audrey Thomas, *Munchmeyer and Prospero on the Island*, Bobbs
   Merrill
Sheila Watson, *The Double Hook*, McClelland & Stewart
Ethel Wilson, *The Equations of Love*; *Hettie Dorval*; *Swamp Angel*,
   Macmillan of Canada

POETRY
Earle Birney, *Selected Poems*, McClelland & Stewart
bill bissett, *killer whale*, Talonbooks; *nobody owns the earth*,
   Anansi
George Bowering, *Touch*, McClelland & Stewart
Audrey Alexandra Brown, *A Dryad in Nanaimo*, McGraw-Hill
   Ryerson
Michael Carmichael, *Oyster Wine*, Island Press
David Day, *The Cowichan*, Oolichan Books
Maxine Gadd, *Guns of the West*, Blew Ointment Press
John Hulcoop, *Three Ring Circus Songs*, Talonbooks
Lionel Kearns, *By the Light of the Silvery McLune*, Daylight
Joy Kogawa, *A Choice of Dreams*, McClelland & Stewart
Patrick Lane, *Beware the Seasons of Fire*, Anansi
Charles Lillard, *Drunk on Wood*, Sono Nis
Dorothy Livesay, *Collected Poems: The Two Seasons*, McGraw-Hill
   Ryerson
Pat Lowther, *This Difficult Flowering*, Very Stone House
Daphne Marlatt, *The Vancouver Poems*, Coach House Press
Susan Musgrave, *Grave-Dirt and Selected Strawberries*, Macmillan
   of Canada
bp nichol, *love: a book of remembrances*, Talonbooks
P.K. Page, *Poems Selected and New*, Anansi

Kevin Roberts, *Cariboo Fishing Notes*, Beau Geste; *West Country*,
  Oolichan Books
Andreas Schroeder, *A File of Uncertainties*; *The Ozone Minataur*,
  Sono Nis
Robin Skelton, *Timelight*, McClelland & Stewart
Tom Wayman, *Waiting for Wayman*, McClelland & Stewart
Phyllis Webb, *Selected Poems*, Talonbooks
J. Michael Yates, *Nothing Speaks for the Blue Moraines*, Sono Nis

BRITISH COLUMBIA MAGAZINES
Canadian Fiction Magazine, Vancouver
Canadian Literature, U.B.C.
Capilano Review, Capilano College
Event, Douglas College
Island, Malaspina College
Malahat Review, U. of Victoria
Prism: International, U.B.C.
Raincoast Chronicles, Madeira Park
West Coast Review, Simon Fraser U.

67 77 87 97 08 18 28 38 48 THB 9 8 7 6 5 4 3 2 1